THE *William Cormack* STORY

Library and Archives Canada Cataloguing in Publication

Title: The William Cormack story : Newfoundland explorer & Beothuk advocate / Ingeborg Marshall.
Names: Marshall, Ingeborg, 1929- author.
Description: Includes bibliographical references and index.
Identifiers: Canadiana 20230141528 | ISBN 9781989417843 (softcover)
Subjects: LCSH: Cormack, W. E. (William Eppes), 1796-1868. | LCSH: Explorers—Newfoundland and   Labrador—Biography. | LCSH: Explorers—Scotland—Biography. | LCSH: Naturalists—Newfoundland and   Labrador—Biography. | LCSH: Naturalists—Scotland—Biography. | LCSH: Newfoundland and Labrador—   Description and travel. | CSH: First Nations—Newfoundland and Labrador—History—19th century. | CSH: First Nations—Newfoundland and Labrador—Social life and customs—19th century. | LCGFT: Biographies.
Classification: LCC FC2172.1.C67 M37 2023 | DDC 971.8/01092—dc23

Published by Boulder Books
Portugal Cove-St. Philip's, Newfoundland and Labrador
www.boulderbooks.ca

Design and layout: Tanya Montini
Editor: Stephanie Porter
Copy editor: Iona Bulgin

Printed in China

We acknowledge the financial support of the Government of Newfoundland and Labrador through the Department of Tourism, Culture, Arts and Recreation.

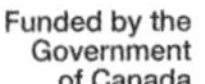

THE *William Cormack* STORY

Newfoundland Explorer & Beothuk Advocate

BOULDER BOOKS

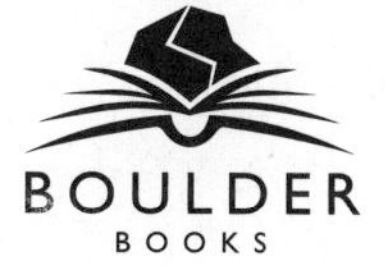

INGEBORG MARSHALL

Table of Contents

Introduction 11

Alexander Cormack and His Family 12

Janet Cormack: The Years 1803–1806 18

William Cormack's Years in Newfoundland
and Scotland, 1806–1818 21

William Cormack's Business Years, 1818–1821 23

Cormack's Plan to Investigate the Interior of Newfoundland 26

Cormack's Trek across Newfoundland in His Own Words:
"Narrative of a Journey across the Island
of Newfoundland in 1822 by W.E. Cormack Esq." 29

Part I   A Trial Expedition: July–August 1822. 29

Part II   Passage from St. John's to Trinity Bay. 37

Part III   Depart from the Sea-coast. 40

Part IV   First View of the Interior—Our Advance into It—
Its Description—Reach the Central Part of the Island. 45

Part V   Continue the Journey into the Western Interior. 57

Part VI   Of the Red Indians and the Other Tribes. 66

Part VII   General Features of the Western Interior, etc. 71

Part VIII   The West Coast. 79

Part IX   American Portion of Newfoundland. 91

Part X   South Coast of Newfoundland—Termination of Journey. 96

Other 19th-Century Travellers through Newfoundland's Interior . . 98

Cormack Returns to Scotland 100

Cormack's Account of His Trek across Newfoundland in 1822 . . . 102

Residence in Newfoundland and Scotland, c.1823–1826 104

Cormack Founds the Boeothick Institution in 1827. 106

Cormack's Trek Inland in Search of Beothuk in November 1827 . 110

Cormack Presents His Report at a Meeting
of the Boeothick Institution. 119

The Search for Beothuk Carried Out by Three Indian Men,
Starting in Spring 1828. 122

Meeting of Members of the Boeothick Institution
on June 24, 1828 124

Shanawdithit Placed under the Care of the Boeothick
Institution in 1828 128

Cormack's Business in St. John's. 141

Cormack Moves to London and Other Maritime Provinces 146

Cormack Moves to Australia in 1836 150

Cormack Moves to New Zealand in 1839 154

Cormack Travels to London in 1843 159

Cormack Returns to New Zealand. 161

Cormack Returns to London 164

Cormack Travels to California during the
Gold Rush, 1851–1858 167

Cormack Moves to British Columbia in 1859 170

Cormack's Legacy in Newfoundland 177

Acknowledgments. 181

Appendix 1   On the natural history and economical uses of
cod, capelin, cuttle-fish, and seal, as they occur on
the Banks of Newfoundland, and the coasts of that
island and Labrador. Communicated in a letter to
Professor Jameson, by W.E. Cormack, Esq. 183

Appendix 2   Memorandum of the locality of the bone of the
Dinornis Giganteus found in the north part of New
Zealand in 1849. For Professor Owen. 195

Endnotes. 199

About the Author 222

List of Illustrations

Figure 1.   Portrait of William Eppes Cormack.

Figure 2.   Steel's New and Correct Chart of the Island of Newfoundland with particular plans of its harbours and manuscript notes by W.E. Cormack, including his route across Newfoundland in 1822, and notes on mineral resources and geology on the west and south coasts.

Figure 3.   Portrait of Shanawdithit.

Figure 4.   Shanawdithit's Sketch I: Captain Buchan's visit to Beothuk camp at Red Indian Lake, where his two marines were killed.

Figure 5.   Shanawdithit's Sketch II: Capture of Demasduit on Red Indian Lake.

Figure 6.   Shanawdithit's Sketch IV: Beothuck camps on Badger Bay River.

Figure 7.   Shanawdithit's Sketch VI: Summer and winter mamateeks, smoking house.

Figure 8.   Shanawdithit's Sketch X: Dwelling house at Roope's Plantation in which she lived, drawn by Shanawdithit, who placed the back and front part next to each other.

Figure 9.   Shanawdithit's Sketch IX: Mythological emblems.

Figure 10.   Cormack's gravestone in the cemetery in New Westminster.

FIGURE 1. PORTRAIT OF WILLIAM EPPES CORMACK.

Introduction

William Eppes[1] Cormack is celebrated for his walk across the interior of the island of Newfoundland in 1822 and for his involvement with the Beothuk: his collection of information about Beothuk history and culture and his attempts to prevent their extinction. Several reports of his interior explorations have been published,[2] and the information he obtained from the Beothuk woman Shanawdithit, the last known member of her people, is an important part of what is known about Beothuk history and culture.[3] Although he is a central figure in Newfoundland's history, surprisingly little is known about Cormack's life, his birth in St. John's, his family's ties to Newfoundland and to Prince Edward Island, his global roaming, and his death in Westminster, BC.

Alexander Cormack and His Family

Alexander Cormack (c.1762–1803), a Protestant Scot, and father of William Eppes Cormack, arrived in St. John's in 1782 at the age of 19. Alexander may have been sent to this outpost as an employee of one of the established Scottish firms in St. John's. There is speculation that he may, for some time, have been a junior partner with the trading firm Hart, Eppes, and Co. Newfoundland was one of Britain's oldest North American possessions and St. John's, a town with about 3,000 inhabitants,[4] the main port of call for the Grand Banks fishery. St. John's was also the third point in a triangular trade that included Europe and the West Indies.

Few details are known about Alexander Cormack's life before his arrival, though the record of his life in St. John's[5] reveals a reliable young man who was, to use the Scottish term, "canny," or capable of making smart decisions in a challenging business environment. By 1791, Cormack had become a well-established member of the town's elite and one of the "Principal Merchants of St. John's" who signed petitions and lobbied governors.[6] He was also a member of the Grand Jury, where he was listed alongside members of the town's largest merchant houses.[7] Cormack's numerous appearances in court as litigant, suing or being sued in cases concerning trade, reflect some of his business interests.

Alexander Cormack was the owner of three vessels: the *Nancy*, the *Rose*, and the *Two Sisters*, and shared ownership of the 55-ton sloop *Betsey* with the St. John's firm Hart, Eppes, and Co.[8] His trade transactions extended to Dartmouth, Quebec City, Prince Edward Island, South America (for molasses), Grenada Island, and Suriname in the West Indies. He seems to have become independent of larger firms.

In 1791, Alexander Cormack married 17-year-old Janet McAuslan (1774–1821). Her father, Robert McAuslan,[9] had come to St. John's from Glasgow with his wife, Grizel (nee Wright), and their three children in 1776.[10] In St. John's, he became involved in the fishery and in 1778 was appointed deputy postmaster of Newfoundland.[11]

Alexander and Janet settled in a rented house in the Third Division, the part of town between Nobles Cove and the Engine House. Janet's parents lived nearby in the Fourth Division. At this time, St. John's was divided into six divisions, running from River Head (west) to Chain Rock (east). The main roads through town were the Lower Path (now Water Street), which followed parallel to the harbour's northern shoreline, and the Upper Path (today's Duckworth Street).

According to the 1794/95 census of St. John's, the Cormacks had one son, called Alexander, and one daughter, whose name is not known.[12] On May 5, 1796, Janet gave birth to another son, whom they named William Eppes in honour of their friend and business associate William Isham Eppes. Three months after William's birth, their son, Alexander, died.[13] Unsanitary conditions prevailed in St. John's and the family was living in the most crowded division of town, a factor that may have contributed to the child's death. Soon after, the Cormacks moved to a residence on the western end of the Second Division, just west of today's Waldegrave Street. William lived there for the first two years of his life.

Alexander Cormack and William Isham Eppes were friends as well as business associates. Eppes had come from Poole, England, where he and his family were associated with the Lesters. Benjamin and Isaac Lester owned some of the largest fishing stations in Placentia and Trinity bays, as well as dozens of ships, many built in Newfoundland. Through Lester's influence, Eppes secured the position of purser in the garrison in St. John's.[14] Eppes was later promoted to Commissary of Provisions, which made him responsible for providing food and other necessities to the hundreds of soldiers stationed in St. John's.[15] He married Elizabeth Randolph and settled in St. John's, where the couple raised two sons and two daughters.[16]

In 1797, Alexander received a grant of a little more than 11 acres of land "about a mile from the [Waterford] river on the north side lying to the westward of Fortune's plantation … to take and keep without being interrupted in the quiet and peaceful enjoyment thereof, so long as he shall continue to occupy the same for the purpose of carrying on the Fishery."[17] Though Cormack's land grant had nothing to do with the fishing trade, the wording of the grant had to conform with British legislation that meant to discourage permanent settlement by people who did not work in the fishery. Cormack had asked for the grant because he wanted to raise cattle for personal consumption and to sell beef. He also leased Fir Hill Farm in Outer Cove, which was accessible by boat.[18] He thereby followed the trend among merchants and garrison officers who purchased or leased land in the immediate vicinity of St. John's for agricultural purposes.[19] This area was known to have good soil and Alexander would have hired servants to do the cultivation and harvest. Governor William Waldegrave promoted farming to alleviate ongoing food shortages in

Newfoundland and encouraged merchants to set up a market and a slaughterhouse.[20]

Food shortages were a major concern at the end of the 18th century, the result of trade sanctions that England and the United States imposed on each other after the American Revolution.[21] The shortage of food also affected the military garrison, and with it the reputation of William Eppes, who was Commissary of Provisions. In December 1797, Eppes reported that a large quantity of spoiled food in storage at the garrison had been dumped into the harbour and that there might not be sufficient supplies for the soldiers for the winter.[22] He shortly afterwards went to England[23] and Alexander Cormack was appointed Acting Commissary in his absence.[24] This placed him in a difficult position. By January 1798, all available food in St. John's had been bought or requisitioned, with only 10 weeks' supply left in the stores.[25] Cormack subsequently spent more than £3,000 to purchase pork, flour, butter, peas, fish, and potatoes from local merchants for the garrison. Waldegrave questioned this expense, but an investigation showed that the receipts were entirely in order.[26]

Alexander Cormack may have overcome Waldegrave's impression that he was extravagant with public funds by volunteering for the Committee for the Relief of the Poor. He also became a member of the committee that raised money for a new Church of England,[27] as the old one was dilapidated. Privately, he purchased a half-share in Roope's Plantation on the harbourfront in the Second Division.[28] The deed describes it as a substantial property "consisting of a Dwelling House, Store, Wharf, Cook Room, Flake and Fish House." Most likely the Cormack family moved to the plantation. It later became William Eppes Cormack's home until he left the province for good.

In 1795, Janet Cormack's brother, Peter McAuslan, bought 1.5 acres (Lot 32) in Prince Edward Island for £23.[29] Peter had done well, farming and trading in real estate. Sometime during 1799 or 1800, Janet and Peter's parents, Robert and Grizel McAuslan, joined Peter in Prince Edward Island. As it turned out, Robert McAuslan was able to purchase town Lot 498 in Charlottetown and secure a land grant for Lot 549 "for no money."[30]

In his capacity as an active member of the St. John's community, Alexander tried to sort out problems with a new grammar school that had opened for the town's Protestant elite. Louis Amadeus Anspach, a Swiss-born clergyman and educator, had been recruited from England on a three-year contract to run the school. But as soon as it opened, there were insufficient funds and discord arose among the subscribers about fees. The affair became so rancorous that Cormack, as treasurer, had to take subscribers to court to pay the schoolmaster and his staff.[31]

By 1800, Alexander and Janet Cormack celebrated the birth of another daughter,[32] Janet Grace Cormack, her second name honouring her grandmother, Grizel, which is Scots Gaelic for Grace.[33] In the following year, they welcomed a baby boy: John Bell Cormack was named after another one of Alexander's merchant friends who was a partner in the company of Cunningham and Bell.[34]

Two years later the Cormacks lost their elder daughter. She is listed in the 1796/97 census of St. John's but was not among the Cormack children who survived into adulthood.[35] The Church of England burial registry for that year lists an unprecedented number of mostly unnamed children who died of unstated causes.[36] Fifty-nine children were buried in 1802, whereas only six children were buried in 1801, and in 1803, when burial records were kept for only six months, there were no entries of children.

Alexander Cormack made his last appearance at the St. John's courthouse on June 28, 1803, on a minor debt matter. Less than a month later, he was no longer alive.[37] His death at age 41 must have been sudden, because he died intestate, that is, without a will.

Janet Cormack: The Years 1803-1806

On August 15, 1803, Janet Cormack made perhaps her first visit to the St. John's courthouse to ask for permission to settle her husband's estate as she wanted to ensure that her husband's possessions were given to her as his rightful heir. She was 29 years old and must have paid attention to her husband's business during their marriage, or she would not have considered administering the estate. It was certainly not typical in this era for a woman to be the sole executrix of a merchant's estate.[38] Luckily for her, it had become customary for widows in Newfoundland to inherit their husband's property when there was no will.[39]

At the court hearing, Janet had to swear that her husband had "died Intestate and without a Will" and was granted the all-important "Letters of Administration" by which she was made executrix of Alexander's estate. The condition was that she return to court within a year to provide "a true and perfect inventory of all the said goods, chattels, and credits of the deceased which already have, or hereafter shall, come into [her] hands."[40] She was also required to post a surety set at £5,000, equal to the estimated value of Alexander's estate, which would be forfeited if she did not follow the court's orders.

As Janet did not have this amount of money, two prominent

Scottish merchants, Richard Reed and David Rennie, who had accompanied her to court, declared their willingness to guarantee the surety "of good and lawful money … made and levied on their goods and chattels."[41] Both men had served on juries and committees with Alexander for almost a decade.[42] There is no evidence that William Eppes came forward to assist.

Janet Cormack returned to court in August 1804 with the required information. The will and probate record revealed that her husband of 12 years had left her well off, but not wealthy: the estate was valued at more than £8,000.[43] While most possessions had been successfully sold, goods valued at £1,500 remained at the store.

With cash in hand, Janet offered George Elliot £560 for his half-share in Roope's Plantation, which he accepted.[44] The sales document states that the property was sold jointly to Janet, widow of the late Alexander Cormack, and to the children of her and her late husband. As executrix, Janet also filed nine writs in court to collect on debts, all of which were paid.[45] Janet also purchased an "enclosed meadow" near Fort William, including tenement or premises with "all the rents, issues, profits and improvements thereto."[46] At the time, Governor Erasmus Gower (1804–1806) hired Thomas George Eastaff to draw up a town plan and mark out a new road, which became today's Gower Street.[47] Janet's land near Fort William would have been suitable for building lots.

Meanwhile, Janet's brother, Peter McAuslan, returned from Prince Edward Island to assist his sister in the long-term task of winding down Alexander's business affairs. He sold shop goods in St. John's and sent some of the goods, along with the usual salt, rum, molasses, and fish, to Prince Edward Island.[48]

In the spring of 1806, young William Eppes Cormack acquired a stepfather, as Janet Cormack agreed to marry David Rennie. Janet travelled with her three children to Edinburgh, where Rennie had moved in the spring. He maintained his partnership with Stuart and Rennie by working in the company's office in Greenock. In 1790, he had joined James Stuart of Scotland to form a company called Stuart & Rennie, the third Scottish firm to establish a permanent trade between Scotland and Newfoundland; it later grew into one of the largest Scottish trading companies.[49] At the time, David had become the firm's St. John's agent.[50] He was 41 years old when he married 32-year-old Janet Cormack.[51]

Sailing from St. John's to Scotland in optimal weather conditions typically took three weeks but could last four or five. This trip to Scotland with his mother and siblings would have been the first time that nine-year-old William had a taste of ocean travel onboard one of the large sailing vessels of the day, an experience he repeated many times during his roving life. Once they disembarked in Greenock, the family would have travelled to Edinburgh by coach. They stayed with John Wright, a relative on Janet's mother's side, who had a shop in the Old City.[52] Before the wedding could take place, Janet had to prove that she had "resided upwards of six weeks in Edinburgh."[53]

David and Janet's marriage ceremony took place on April 23, 1806, and was entered in St. Cuthbert's Parish register as: "David Rennie, Merchant, St. Andrews Church Parish, and Janet McAuslan or Cormack, St. Cuthbert's Parish, relict of Alexander Cormack.[54]

William Cormack's Years in Newfoundland and Scotland, 1806-1818

By the fall of 1806, David Rennie took his family back to St. John's, continuing to be the Newfoundland agent for Stuart & Rennie.[55] They may have moved into a property later known as "Castle Rennie," which faced Signal Hill Road and included a dwelling house and outbuildings, "trees, woods, gardens, and waterways."[56] Castle Rennie became a St. John's landmark well beyond Rennie's time in Newfoundland.[57] (The current St. Joseph's Convent on Signal Hill Road is believed to have been built on the precincts of Castle Rennie.) Rennie once again served on the Grand Jury.[58]

In 1807, Janet gave birth to David Stuart Rennie, named after her husband. A second son, born in 1809, called James, received the middle name Gower in honour of Governor Erasmus Gower.[59] With two more sons added to the family, the problems of finding good health services and educational opportunities may have become acute. Deteriorating social services and living conditions in St. John's may have led to the decision to return to Scotland. St. John's had "no system of education … or hospitals, sanitation, organized road systems, or fire services."[60] In 1810, Janet was expecting another child and this may have been the catalyst for the couple to leave Newfoundland, since David Rennie could conduct business on either side of the Atlantic. Janet kept the properties she had acquired as a legacy for Alexander's children, William Eppes, Janet Grace, and John Bell Cormack, renting out the properties during her absence.

Prince Edward Island became another focus of business for the Rennie-Cormack family, possibly inspired by Peter McAuslan's experiences. In 1810, David Rennie purchased Lot 23 northwest of Charlottetown. The land fronted on the Gulf of St. Lawrence and included the area where New Glasgow was later established.[61] The island had opened large areas for development, which were often purchased by absentee landlords who, in turn, attracted settlers willing to clear the forest and cultivate the land.[62]

On their arrival in Scotland, the Rennie family settled in Glasgow, though David probably maintained an office in Greenock. In September, Janet gave birth to a baby girl, christened Janet Emma Rennie.[63] In the following years, the Rennies welcomed two more boys: William Frederick Rennie, born in February 1812,[64] and Robert Rennie, born in April 1814.[65]

The Rennie family made use of the fine educational opportunities offered in Glasgow and Edinburgh. William Eppes Cormack, aged 15 in May 1811, attended Glasgow University to study Greek, a language required for a classical education. In 1813/14, he studied "Logica."[66] At Edinburgh University, he attended classes in the natural sciences, particularly geology and mineralogy, under the well-known scholar Professor Robert Jameson, who later became his mentor.[67] His brothers attended Glasgow University and Edinburgh University as well.[68]

In 1828, when William Eppes Cormack was 22 years old, his stepfather, David Rennie, considered him ready to take over part of his business. He was to go to Prince Edward Island to ready Lot 23 for the arrival of Scottish settlers, which meant dividing the land into parcels of between 90 and 150 acres. He also had to organize the harvest of pine and hardwood for export.[69] In addition, Cormack purchased 5 acres of land at the south side of Rustico Bay on his own account. In 1819, David Rennie gave William power of attorney,[70] thereby authorizing him "to sell and dispose of land" and to sort out disputes which had arisen with tenants.

By May 1820, 285 settlers had arrived in Prince Edward Island.[71] Being very resourceful, Cormack supplied them with their needs, which they did not have to repay, so that they would labour on their lot and not have to work for cash elsewhere. This was to make them feel attached to their land, and they ultimately repaid in rent increases as the land became more valuable through the improvements.[72] In a retrospective, one of the early pioneers recalled that the settlers were not only clearing the land for cultivating crops but also were selling the lumber and building ships.[73]

Even before the arrival of settlers, Cormack was in Charlottetown to serve on a 12-man jury[74] and in 1820 was named to "a new

Commission of the Peace."[75] He was also reappointed as a magistrate.[76] As a male between 16 and 60 years of age, Cormack was obligated to bear arms and attend military musters and exercises in the volunteer militia. He was finally assigned to the Queens County Regiment as Captain of the Grenadier Company at Rustico in the 1st Battalion.[77]

The settlement of Lot 23 in time became one of the most populated sections in the province.[78] Cormack was able to resolve outstanding disputes about occupancy and arrears of rent, though in some cases he had to take a tenant to court to collect debts.[79] Cormack also purchased parcels of land on his own account. Peter McAuslan sold him Lots 470, 549, and 556 in the Royalty of Charlottetown.[80] Cormack later purchased a further six pasture lots, totalling 72 acres,[81] and half of town Lots 8 and 9 in Charlottetown.[82] Although Cormack was successfully integrated into the business and civic life of Prince Edward Island, in 1821 he followed other plans.

In June 1821, Cormack learned of his beloved mother's death of anemia.[83] She was 46 years old and was outlived by eight of her 10 children. William Eppes left Prince Edward Island sometime in the following winter to return to St. John's, the place of his birth, where he had spent his early childhood years. He was 25 years old and ready to attend to business interests in connection with family properties in St. John's, which his mother had placed into a trust disposition for the three Cormack children: William Eppes, Janet Grace, and John Bell.[84]

The largest and most valuable holding was the waterfront property, Roope's Plantation. William Cormack appears to have lived in the spacious dwelling at Roope's but probably sublet some of its wharf and storage facilities. Roope's Plantation also incorporated large tracts of land between Water and New Gower streets, as shown on the Plan of St. John's by surveyor William R. Noad.[85] Due to housing shortages in St. John's during the early 1800s, some of the land was sold as building lots and would have yielded ground rents.[86] The Cormack siblings also owned the River Head Farm, which their father had purchased for raising cattle,[87] and a field with "tenements" near Fort William,[88] 3.5 acres of Crown land that Janet Cormack had leased for 21 years,[89] in addition to substantial acreage in the area of today's Victoria Park.[90]

Cormack's Plan to Investigate the Interior of Newfoundland

Once Cormack had settled at Roope's Plantation, merchant colleagues of his father and stepfather are likely to have offered their help with setting up a proper merchant house and suggesting goods and customers in St. John's and abroad. However, starting a business was far from William Eppes Cormack's mind. He wanted to explore the interior of Newfoundland. Considering himself free from professional engagements, his aim was to "penetrate through the central part of the Island."[91] When he described the objective of his expedition to Governor Charles Hamilton, he stated that he wanted to obtain some knowledge of the interior of the country and did not mention an interest in the Beothuk.

Having witnessed the opportunities in Prince Edward Island as it opened its forested inland areas to settlement and cultivation, Cormack was most likely interested in investigating what Newfoundland's interior had to offer. It was virtually unexplored by Europeans, and he wished to find out about "its natural conditions and geography."[92] As Cormack possessed considerable drive, perseverance, and courage, he felt ready and able to undertake the hazardous journey of crossing the island on foot.

Though it has generally been assumed that the main purpose

of Cormack's trek was to meet with the Beothuk, the evidence suggests otherwise. When choosing a route, Cormack was guided by the assumption that the "natural characteristics of the interior were most decidedly exhibited between Trinity Bay on the east coast and St. George's Bay on the west."[93] He, therefore, planned to "traverse the main body of the island at its widest, excluding all large peninsulas."[94] With regard to making contact with the Beothuk, Cormack believed he would come across some of them on their route since Captain David Buchan had reported that they occupied the whole of the "central parts."[95]

Cormack's plan for the expedition may also have been inspired by John Barrow's *Chronological History of Voyages into the Arctic Regions,* which includes Buchan's[96] report of his expedition to Red Indian Lake in central Newfoundland in January 1811.[97] According to Buchan, "the general face of the country in the interior exhibits a mountainous appearance, with rivers, ponds, and marshes in the intermediate levels or valleys." He found most of its timber stunted. Barrow noted that "we know so little of the interior [of Newfoundland], or even of its shores" after a settlement of more than 200 years, and no attempt has yet been made "to collect a Flora of the island."[98] In 1823, following his journey, Cormack submitted the first report of his expedition to Barrow and intended "to continue to pursue his enquiries into the natural production of the country," informing Barrow of anything "worthy of being communicated" in the future.[99] Cormack's interest in geology was inspired by his mentor and "excellent friend and distinguished promoter of science and enterprise," Professor Robert Jameson, at Edinburgh University,[100] who later helped him identify the rocks he had collected on his trek.[101]

"To accompany me in the performance, I engaged into my service, first a Mikmak Indian, and next a European whom I thought fitted." This European was Charles Fox Bennett (later prime minister of Newfoundland), a friend from his childhood days in St. John's, whom Cormack trusted in every respect. Of volunteers, there had been several, but Cormack did not believe that they would have been equal to the task. Cormack's Mi'kmaq guide, Joseph Sylvester, came from Bay d'Espoir, in particular the area near Weasel Island, to which Sylvester planned to return after the trek to join close kinsfolk.[102] Although today Cormack's guide is also referred to as Sylvester Joe,[103] Cormack said that his name was Joseph Sylvester and he usually referred to him as "Joe," "Sylvester," or "my Indian."[104] Since Cormack was not conversant with the Mi'kmaq language, it is assumed that Sylvester spoke English and possibly some French. Regarding his skills, he was not only a good shot but also an experienced woodsman who knew how to travel and survive with a minimum of support in the type of country that they planned to cross.

Cormack's Trek across Newfoundland in His Own Words

"Narrative of a Journey across the Island of Newfoundland in 1822 by W.E. Cormack Esq."

Before leaving on his trek, Cormack was to train himself and his Indian to try his fidelity by making an excursion from St. John's to Placentia and back that would last from July 25 to August 19, 1822.[105] Cormack thereby also ascertained the necessary equipment and discovered that it would be impossible to travel in the "totally unknown interior until subsistence could be procured there, the supply of which is extremely precarious until berries are ripening, and the wild birds and beasts have left their birth-places to roam at large and are likely to fall in the traveller's way."[106]

At the end of August, Cormack had equipped his two men with everything necessary for a three-month campaign and considered his party sufficient.[107] However, just before leaving, he was told that the chief government authority was opposed to his project and, in consequence, Cormack was deprived of the services of Charles Fox Bennett, who was a stipendiary by local appointment and could not accompany him without the governor's permission.

Excerpts (some of which are paraphrased) from Cormack's diary follow.

Part I. A Trial Expedition: July–August 1822

July 25th. Thursday: In the evening arrived at Portugal Cove, a typical out harbour, as the inhabitants are all employed in the fishery, and all buildings relate to it. There is no storekeeper, all planters are getting their supplies from St. John's, Harbour Grace, and Portugal Cove.

On the 26th walked to Chamberlain, the path led through a marsh and afterwards along the shore; came through Broad Cove and Topsail.

July 27th. Saturday: Walked from Topsail to Kelligrews along the beach, about 4 miles. Reached Tilly at Kelligrews in the morning where we breakfasted and prepared for leaving human habitation for a few days. Left Kelligrews about noon for the Barren Hills, a distance of 5 miles, and camped for the night at the north end of a small lake.

About three miles in had an adventure—stopped to change my gun for bear when Joe disappeared: when ready to proceed after loading called for Joe but no answer, discharged my gun but of no use: then concluded he has deserted and determined after wasting an hour on that spot if he did not appear I would return to Kelligrews and proceed to Holyrood by water then hire a man to go with me to Placentia. I had my gun in my hand to discharge for the last time as a signal of departure when Joe appeared, having gone ahead a little and sat down to wait by a murmuring brook which prevented him hearing me. Saw Bear and Deer tracks in abundance in the marshes and along the edges of ponds.

July 28th. Sunday: Left our place of encampment mid-day. We steered between two large irregular lakes. From a hill which we take to be the soldier's lookout have a great view.

Being foggy we travelled by compass about 4 miles. Encamped at the edge of a lake and cooked a supper of Partridge.

July 29th. Monday: On the following day we walked for about 6 miles through the "Flaky Downs" and reached Holyrood at dusk. Put up at Mr. Ezekiel. Having bathed in the lake at 6 o'clock in the morning then walked almost continuously nearly tired us out.

July 30th. Tuesday: The following morning Mr. Ezekiel affronted Joe so much that he was going to desert me now in earnest. He had his hat on and his blanket tied up for the purpose, however I pacified him after a good deal of persuasion. Moved on to Mr. Connell, also at Holyrood, who paid every attention; invited us for dinner and had us sleep at his house.

July 31st. Left Mr. Connell's before noon and had Tom Fennel guide us to the first "Flaky Down" about 3 miles S of Holyrood. Shot two braces of partridge. We encamped for the night in a small gully among its bushes. Bear and deer tracks seen almost every where on our route. Signs of beaver & otter.

August 1st. Thursday: Proceeded on to the second "Flaky Down." The country southward becomes clearer of woods and the land south of this is very barren. We proceeded westward. A road to Placentia from St. John's should pass by the S end of the 2nd or 3rd "Flaky Down," though a considerable part of the road must pass through intervals of wood & brush & marshes alternately. [It must be assumed that before setting out on his trip, Cormack had been asked to assess where a road from St. John's to Placentia could be made.]

August 2nd. Friday: We took our departure about 10 o'clock

a.m. and made the best of our way through woods and marshes westward. About 2 p.m. we unexpectedly came upon a pond with a Beaver house and 2 Beaver but shot none of them. Crossing a shallow river, I fell off the rocks and sustained damage by wetting my gun and hurting my knee. The river had large quantities of the fresh cockle or oyster. Having followed a westerly string of marshes we observed a wolf track on the Deer path we were following across a marsh. The last 3½ miles walk on this day led thro very woody land which made the walk very unpleasant.

August 3rd. Saturday: Left our encampment of last night near a small lake from which we saw the Blue Hills for the first time. During the last two days we only proceeded about 1½ miles as our way was very impeded with ponds. About 5 p.m. ascended a tree to look at the country before us, saw a large Deer at the edge of a lake; Joe went to the extremity of the pond for a chance of a shot at him. It was in vain.

August 4th. Sunday: Marched thro the woods about 4 miles and halted on the edge of a beautiful lake before cooking Breakfast. We were hoping it would be the last but two till reaching Placentia as our stock of provisions had diminished considerably. Discovered an inhabited beaver house: Joe succeeded in feeling one underground with his stick. Caught it by the hind legs and dragged it out of its hole. I killed it with the axe as soon as his head appeared. Joe cut him open, took out its guts and stomach & pulled out its contents with his hand, turned the latter inside out and plaited it in a Drummers plait, without any other cleaning. Roasting was done by throwing the mutton on the brands of burning wood and turning it once or twice. We did not spare the beaver, both as a solid & in form of soup. It was delicious, more like mutton than any other meat but of a much finer flavour.

August 5th. Monday: Resolute to remain at our encampment today to recruit & feast on beaver. During an excursion near our camp killed 4 ducks and 4 geese: the 4 ducks at one shot.

August 6th. Tuesday: The weather foggy and wet all morning. It rained considerably during the night, but we were guarded against it by having erected a sort of horizontal plane and laying our blanket out to windward which was a sufficient protection against all weather. We have three days journey before us yet, 6 to 10 miles a day is as much as can be accomplished. Stepping over stumps of trees, the rocky ground, up and down hills, looking for the best way to avoid ponds and having to go round them retards the traveller in making a straight course: one mile of it is as laborious as four on a road. Ascended the highest land between Holyrood & the Blue Hills of Placentia: On descending followed a barren and after 2 miles came upon woods and encamped there for the night.

August 7th. Wednesday: Rained all night but we were protected by our camp with blanket to windward. Proceeding half a mile from our camp saw the sea within 2 miles of SW. First took it for Placentia Bay but it proved to be St. Mary's. The country now assumed a more open appearance, crossed a small river running S into St. Mary's Bay. Anywhere in this neighbourhood within 2 miles of this part of St. Mary's Bay appears favourable for a road from Placentia as the land here is much clearer than that north of it.

August 8th. Thursday: Felled a tree to cross the stream we encamped as to proceed on our journey WNW. Ascended the highland and got within 3½ miles of the NE arm of Placentia Harbour when we encamped for the night in a small wood. The land here is barer than any we met with.

Taking a view of the whole country from hence to St. John's, the best track for a road is to Holyrood nearly the course which we have come but instead of going by Portugal Cove it should take its course by the Kelligrews barrens. In this way cutting through woods is avoided and is shorter.

August 9th. Friday: Reached the head of the NE arm of Placentia about midday and made for the first house on the opposite side of the arm. There we found a sort of farm and one man, Mr. John Bland, servant of the crown, notary of Placentia. He gave us what he had to eat, bread, butter, & pork.

The salmon fishery has been over for 10 days past. We had to walk down to Placentia along the beach. To our disappointment learned that the H.M.S. Ranger has left Placentia the day before. Put up at Mrs. Newman's, a comfortable house for the country. In Placentia, the French capital, remains of forts are still visible.

Mr. Sweetman's farm has 35 acres of what may be arable land; the place is stocked with about 50 dairies (cows). All are fishermen here, except a few families as Sweetmans, Bradshaws, Blackburns & the Priest Cleary; Sweetman the only and principal merchant. Not one tenth of the former business here.

August 10th. Saturday: Called on Mr. Sweetman and visited his farm with him. Called on Capt. Withers at Mr. Blackburn's in the morning. People here pay considerable attention to raising potatoes, beets, & cattle and to gardening.

August 11th. Sunday: Dined at Mr. Sweetman's with Father Cleary, Doctor Bradshaw and domestics. Capt. Warren, Mr. Walsh and Mr. Carey spent remainder of the day there.

August 12th. Monday: Attended Capt. Withers' sale of the Concord, bought by Mr. Sweetman for 90 pound sterling. Dined with Mr. Sweetman, went by water in his punt to Mr. Green's farm at Cape Verd, spent evening with Mr. S. and Dr. Bradshaw. Mr. Sweetman collected [from other fishermen] about 8,000 QTLs. fish this year and made himself about 6,000. All his dealers are within 2 miles of him; he could double his collection.

August 13th. Tuesday: Dined with Mr. Sweetman. Left Placentia about 6 o'clock in Mr. S. punt & reached head of NE arm.

August 14th. Wednesday: Left at 5 o'clock in the morning, having slept in the farmhouse of Blanch's of Placentia. Had breakfast south of the Blue Hills. The fishing at Placentia is very good. Boats Jacks & 1 Gallopper came in last night loaded, an extraordinary thing so early in the week. Steered from the W Blue Hill through a string of marshes towards New Harbour in Trinity Bay, leaving Spreading Eagle Hill on our left. From this Blue Hill we could see St. Mary's Bay and Trinity Bay with the shore up by Random (Island?). Also the hills about Little Placentia and Port DeGrave with other parts of Conception Bay. Towards the evening fell in with a marsh abounding with the largest and finest bakeapples I ever saw; Joe acknowledged the same; encamped in a wood near this spot. 14 miles.

August 15th. Thursday: Proceed towards Spread Eagle Hill, which we leave on our left. Bay of Despair, up the Bay de Nord about 16 m NE of Grand Jarvis. There is said to be a cross composed of stones regularly laid in a flat rock about 30 ft. long and 20 broad, said to be ancient, ¾ m from the Salt Water.

August 16th. Friday: New Harbour, a fishing settlement, where we arrived after sunset. Proceed on towards Spaniard's Bay, slept 3 miles from it in the woods.

August 17th. Saturday: Had breakfast at Mr. Collins in Spaniard's Bay. Dined at Mr. Danson's with Miss Row and Mr. Samuel Prowse. Met Parsons Lee, Burt & Mr. Campbell there in the evening. Slept at Foxes, a good, clean house, and people very civil.

August 19th. Sunday: Called on by Mr. Ed. Danson & Mr. S. Prowse. See more inhabitants of Spaniard's Bay. Went on a boat with Miss Betsy McKie & Miss Gaden for Portugal Cove. Walked with the ladies and Thos. Gaden to St. John's which we reached about 10 pm.

The trek was a success for Cormack in that it demonstrated Sylvester's capabilities and their compatibility. Cormack also discovered "that it would be impossible to travel in the totally unknown interior until sustenance could be procured there, the supply of food sources is extremely precarious until the berries are ripening, and the wild birds and beasts have left their birth-places to roam at large and are likely to fall in the traveller's way."

Regarding his outfit, Cormack noted "that the traveller who was to cross this country should wear knee-breeches, Esquimaux boots with moccasin feet with one pair of spare soles instead of shoes, and a cap and not a hat. The traveller should avoid canvas trousers as they are stiff and make walking difficult and prevent the free bending of the knee."

Cormack was also able to give advice about the feasibility of a road from St. John's to Placentia. On the request of Lieutenant Mumbee, he submitted a sketch of the lay of the land with his route marked on it and suggested that a road should be close to his route but not lead via Portugal Cove.[108]

The idea of building a road from St. John's to Placentia had been promoted by Captain Stewart, Prince Edward Island, who suggested that Prince Edward Island produce such as bread, flour, and potatoes as well as sheep and cattle could be brought to Newfoundland less costly by off-loading them at Placentia, since it would avoid the perilous route around the Avalon Peninsula to St. John's. He had sent a pamphlet describing such a project to Earl Bathurst, Secretary of State for the Colonies, who had it investigated with regard to its practicability and expense. Considering the dilapidated state of the old forts in St. John's and other projects that needed to be attended to, the building of the road appeared to be less urgent and was eventually turned down.[109]

Part II. Passage from St. John's to Trinity Bay

In the following pages, Cormack and Sylvester's trek across the island is described in Cormack's words, as published in 1915 by J.P. Howley in *The Beothucks or Red Indians*.[110] Lengthy passages about rock formations, mineralogy, and plants are omitted. Detailed descriptions of animals and birds, of the landscape and their trek, are usually abbreviated to remain within the scope of this book.

The proper season had arrived in which to set off, and I embarked at St. John's for Trinity Bay, previously taking with me my Indian only. Uncertainty of result waved over my determination, now more settled (by opposition) to perform at all hazards what I had set out upon. That no one would be injured by my annihilation was a cheering triumph at such a moment.

Cormack's strange statement may have referred to the recent death of his mother, with whom he, as the oldest of her children, most likely had a very warm relationship. He probably believed that his mother would have been the only person to be deeply hurt if his trek had led to his death.

A debatable second explanation for Cormack's belief that nobody would be hurt if his expedition was to lead to his death was, according to a newspaper account, a recent marriage partner, since the marriage had ended in tragedy and psychological trauma. This supposition is based on a story known as "Hunter's Grave," first published in an "old Charlottetown newspaper" in 1879 and republished in the Charlottetown *Guardian* in 1939.[111] Some of Cormack's reported activities and credentials were described fairly accurately, though the given time frame does not fit. According to this tale, Cormack was to marry a Marion Whittier from Rustico, Prince Edward Island. She had once been betrothed to Arthur Hunter, who was thought to have died during the War of 1812. Hunter, however, turned up on the wedding day and, realizing the situation, disappeared into the woods. Desperate and guilt-ridden, Marion led a search party but failed to find him. Hunter's remains were later found by lumbermen and were buried near the river subsequently known as "Hunter's River." Although the story is tenable, there are few proven facts: neither Whittier nor

Hunter could be found in existing records and the Hunter River was named by surveyor Samuel Holland after a Thomas Orby Hunter, in 1765.[112] To continue in Cormack's words:

On the 30th of August we sailed past Conception Bay, the most populous and important district in Newfoundland. On the promontory between Conception and Trinity bays is the Point of Grates, and close to it Baccalao Island which is famous for the number of sea fowl that frequent it in the breeding season. It is visited by men called Eggers, who carry off cargoes of newly laid eggs of Penguins, once numerous on this coast, but now considered as extirpated, for none have been seen for many years past.

The wind having been unfavourable, it was not until the 31st of August we arrived at Bonaventure, a small fishing harbour on the west side of Trinity Bay. None of the inhabitants here or in the vicinity, as at other Parts of Newfoundland, could give any information about the interior never having been further from the salt water than in pursuit of animals for their furs, and for wood-stuff to build vessels and fishing boats.

September 3rd. Having engaged a boat to carry us to the most inland part of Random Sound, we left Bonaventure for Random Bar, at the western extremity of the Sound. In consequence of black birch and white pine having been produced in this part in considerable quantities for ship building, it appears to have been formerly much resorted to, and vessels have been built there.

September 5th. Our boat having lain dry on the bar nearly all night, we slept in her in preference to encamping in the woods.

My travelling equipment being landed, the boat left us on her return to Bonaventure. An abyss of difficulties instantly sprang up in the imagination between us and the centre of the *Terra Incognita*. That we might be eaten up by packs of wolves was more than probable to the farewell forebodings of the inhabitants we had last seen, if we should escape the Red Indians.

Part III. Depart from the Sea-coast

We put our knapsacks and equipment in order. I wore a grey moleskin shooting jacket, and small clothes of worsted cord, took three entire inside woollen body dresses, worsted stockings and socks, Canadian long moccasin boots. The Indian wore leggings or gaiters made of swanskin blanketing, together with moccasins instead of boots. I was armed with a double-barrelled fowling piece and a brace of bayonetted pistols, two pounds and a half of gunpowder, and ten pounds of bullet and shot. The Indian had a single-barrelled fowling piece and a pistol, and the like quantity of powder and shot. Our stock consisted of a hatchet, two small tin kettles for cooking; about twenty pounds of biscuit, eight pounds of pork, some portable soup, tea and sugar, pepper, salt etc. a blanket each and one for the camp roof, a telescope, a pocket compass each: I took a small fishing rod and tackle, and various minor articles for our casual necessities and for mineralogical and other purposes of observation and notes. On another journey of the kind I should very little vary this equipment.

Cormack had also taken with him the lower part of *Steel's New and Correct Chart of the Island of Newfoundland with Particular Plans of Its Harbours on a Large Scale with an Estimated Scale of 1:675,000, Compiled from Recent Authorities* (1817)[113] (Figure 2). Added on the chart, presumably with Sylvester's help, was a river system from the south coast, at Bay d'Espoir, to Bonavista Bay, which was most likely Sylvester's hunting area. Sylvester probably also knew Peter Sylvester from King's Cove, Bonavista Bay, who may even have been a relative.[114] Once they were on their way, Cormack used the chart to mark their route with a dotted line, starting at St. John's harbour and ending at St. George's Bay. Little flags, intersecting the line between each date, indicated the distance covered on each particular day. With only a pocket compass to determine their course, Cormack was only able to ascertain their route in a general way.

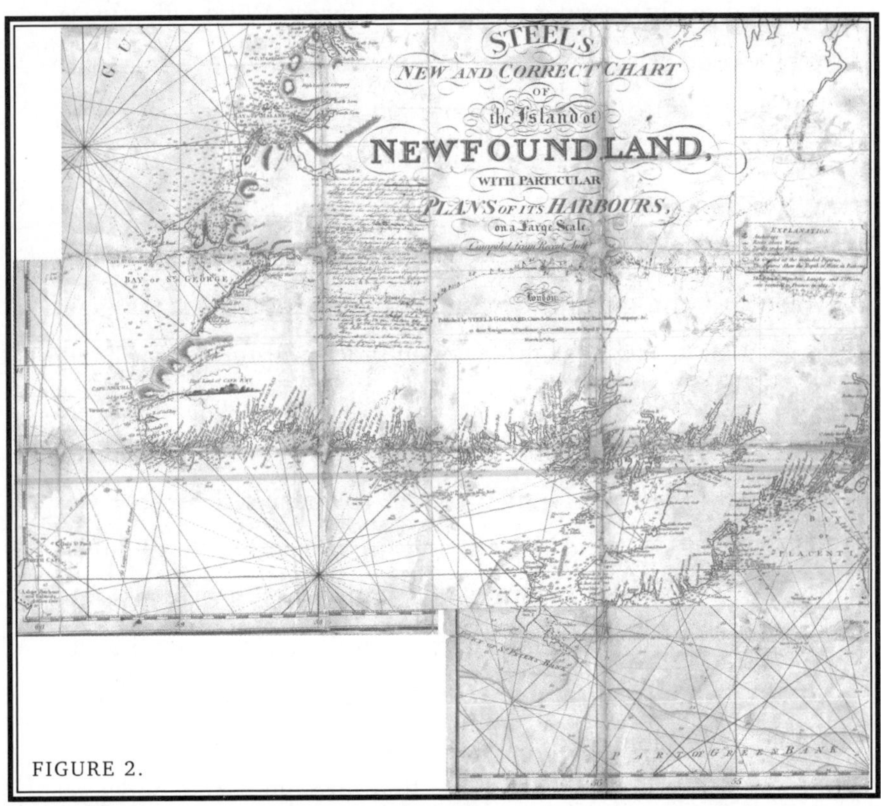

FIGURE 2.

We left this island part of the seashore in a northern direction. The centre of the island bore nearly west from us. After several hours of hard labour, owing chiefly to the great weight of our knapsacks, we made only about two miles progress. At sunset we halted and bivouacked beneath the forest. As the weather was fine, and no prospect of rain, our camp consisted merely of a fire and a bundle of spruce boughs to lie on. My Indian, Joseph Sylvester by name, at midnight rolled himself up in his blanket, and evidently slept perfectly at home.

September 6th. No clear ground appearing in our course, we struck directly westward through the forest. Wind-fallen trees, underwood, and brooks lay in our way which together with the suffocating heat in the woods, and moshetos [mosquitoes], hindered us from advancing more than five miles to-day, in a WNW direction.

September 7th, 8th, 9th. We were occupied in travelling westward through the forest, at the rate of seven or eight miles a day. Marshes and lakes lie hidden in the forest. Every marsh is accompanied almost invariably by a lake, and every hill also by a lake of proportional extent at its foot and the three are frequently found together. The heat in the woods was very oppressive, and there being no circulation of air under the trees, myriads of moshetos, with black and sand flies, annoyed us. There being neither browse, grass, nor berries in any quantity in the pine forest, even traces of any kind of game are seldom seen. Hence the necessity of carrying a stock of provisions to last while travelling through such woods, yet a heavy load prevents expedition and observing much of the natural condition of the country.

The brooks are only visited by otters, the pools and small lakes by beavers and musk rats. The martin is sometimes seen on the trees. Of the feathered tribe, the jay and sometimes the titmouse followed us, chattering and fluttering, shewing that their retreats were never invaded by man. A woodpecker, of which there are two or three kinds, is now and then heard tapping, and sometimes the distant croak of a raven catches the ear. These are the only interruptions to the dead silence that always and everywhere reigns during the day in such forests. The loud notes of the loon, discovered by us at night, as we lay in our camp, in what direction the lakes lay that were near, and we thus avoided them, if in our course next day.

We lodged at nights under the thickest of the woods, encamping or bivouacking in the Indian manner. To make a camp after a day's hard fatigue requires about an hour, and the whole should be done before it is dark. Then, and not till then is it proper to sit down to rest. After supper, each when disposed rolls himself up in his blanket and reposes on his fragrant bed of boughs, placing the soles of the feet near the fire. This precaution the Indian strictly adheres to, as a preservation of health, the feet being wet all day. Apprehensions and thoughts of no ordinary kind occupy the mind unaccustomed to the untrodden boundless wilderness.

September 10th. From the first we had now and then crossed over marshes and open rocky spots in the forest. As we advanced these latter became more frequent. The change of sylvan scenery as we passed from one to another was enlivening and interesting and afforded the luxury of a breeze that freed us from the host of blood-thirsty flies. Early in the day, the ground descending, we came unexpectedly to a rivulet about seventy yards wide, running rapidly over a rocky bed to the north-east, which we forded. It abounded with fine trout, some of which we caught. The roaring of a cataract of some magnitude was heard in the north-east. From the position and course of this stream, we inferred that it was a branch of the river which runs into Clode Sound, in Bonavista Bay.

Leaving the rivulet, the land had a considerable rise for several miles. The trees became larger and stood apart; and we entered upon spacious tracks of rocky ground, entirely clear of wood. Everything indicated our approach to the verge of a country different from the past. We soon found that we were on a great granitic ridge, covered with scattered trees and a variety of beautiful lichens or reindeer moss, partridge berries and whortleberries loaded the ground. Grouse, the indigenous game bird of the country, rose in coveys in every direction, and snipes from every marsh. The birds of passage, ducks, and geese, were flying over us to and fro from their breeding places in the interior and the seacoast; tracks of deer, of wolves fearfully large, of bears, foxes and martens, were seen everywhere. On looking back towards the seacoast, the scene was magnificent.

Part IV. First View of the Interior—Our Advance into It—Its Description—Reach the Central Part of the Island

To the westward, to our inexpressible delight, the interior broke in sublimity before us. What a contrast did this present to the conjectures entertained of Newfoundland! The hitherto mysterious interior lay unfolded below us, a boundless scene, emerald surface, a vast basin. The eye strides again and again over a succession of northerly and southerly ranges of green plains, marbled with woods and lakes of every form and extent, a picture of all the luxurious scenes of national cultivation, receding into invisibleness. The imagination hovers in the distance and clings involuntarily to the undulating horizon of vapour, far into the west, until it is lost. A new world seemed to invite us onward, or rather we claimed the dominion and were impatient to proceed to take possession. Fancy carried us swiftly across the Island.

It was manifested on every hand that this was the season of the year when the earth here offers her stores of productions; land berries were ripening, game birds were fledging, and beasts were emerging to prey upon each other. We consumed unsparingly our remaining provisions, confident that henceforward, with our personal powers, which felt increased by the nature of the objects that presented themselves, aided by what now seemed by contrast the admirable power of our firearms, the destruction of one creature would afford us nourishment and vigour for the destruction of others. There was no will but ours. Thoughts of the aborigines did not alter our determination to meet them, as well as everything living, that might present itself in a country yet untrodden, and before unseen by civilized man. I now adopted, as well for self-preservation as for the sake of accomplishing the object of my excursion, the self-dependent mode of life of the Indian both in spirit and action.

But to look around before we advance. The great exterior features of the eastern portion of the main body of the island are seen from these commanding heights. Overland communication between the bays of the east, north, and south coasts, it appears, might be easily established. The chief obstacles to overcome, as far as regards the mere way, seem to lie in the crossing the mountain belt of twenty or forty miles wide, on which we stood, in order to reach the open low interior. The nucleus of this belt is exhibited in the form of a semi-circular chain of isolated paps and round-backed granitic hills, generally lying north-east and south-west of each other in the rear of Bonavista, Trinity, Placentia, and Fortune Bays. To the southward of us, in the direction of Piper's Hole, in Placentia Bay, one of these conical hills, very conspicuous, I named Mount Clarence, in honour of His Royal Highness, who, when in the nave, had been in Placentia Bay. Our view extended more than forty miles in all directions.

September 11th. We descended into the bosom of the interior. The plains which shone so brilliantly are steppes or savannas, composed of fine black compact peat mould, formed by the growth and decay of mosses. They are in the form of extensive gently undulating beds, stretching northward and southward, with running waters and lakes, skirted with woods, lying between them. They are checkered everywhere upon the surface by deep beaten deer paths, and are magnificent naturel deer parks, adorned by woods and water. It is impossible to describe the grandeur and richness of the scenery, and which will probably remain long undefaced by the hand of man. In vain were associations; in vain did the eye wander for the cattle, the cottage, and the flocks.

Our progress over the savanna country was attended with great labour, and consequently slow, being only the rate of five to seven miles a day to the westward, while the distance walked was equivalent to three or four times as much. Always inclining our course to the westward, we traversed in every direction, partly from choice, to view and examine the country, and partly from the necessity to get round the extremities of lakes and woods, and to look for game for subsistence. One of the most striking features of the interior are the innumerable deer paths on the savannas. They are narrow and take directions as various as the winds, giving the whole country a chequered appearance. Of the millions of acres here, there is no one spot exceeding a few superficial yards that is not bounded on all sides by deer paths.

We however met only small herds of deer as the savannas and plains are during the summer season deserted by them for the mountains in the west part of the island. The Newfoundland deer, and there is only one species in the Island, is a variety of the reindeer, or Carriboo; and that animal in every other country is migratory, always changing place with the seasons for sake of its favourite kind of food. Although they migrate in herds, they travel in files, with their heads to windward, in order that they may, by the scent, discover their enemies, the wolves; their senses of smelling and hearing are very acute. But they are an easy pray to the hunter.

The Beaver. Owing to the presence of the birch tree, all the brooks and lakes in the basin of the interior have been formerly and many are still inhabited by beavers, but these have in many places been destroyed by the Indians. The bark of the birch tree, together with that of a dwarf willow which abounds at the edges of the waters, is the favourite food of the beavers. They obtain the bark of trees by gnawing the trunks through about two feet above the ground, causing them to fall. Some of the trees thus brought to the ground were fifteen inches and upwards in diameter. The tree being felled every branch becomes accessible and by subdividing, portable.

The sagacity displayed by the beavers in constructing their houses has been often described, but it is in their damming operations that their reason is displayed. On witnessing the extent of work performed on some of these dams it is difficult to persuade oneself that it has not been done by man. The materials used are trunks of trees, mud, sticks, and stones. Their houses are formed of the same materials and resemble in their exterior a hemispherical mud-hovel from eight to ten feet in length, but without a visible door or aperture for the escape of smoke. They have different abodes for summer and winter, occupying the former for four to five months, and the latter seven or eight months of the year, the latter being larger and more substantial. The chief entrance of both is under the surface of the water in the lake. A house has often another entrance at the back or land side if the ground will permit, also under water for egress and ingress to and from the adjoining woods.

A family, which generally consists of two old, and two, three, or four young, will commence early in September to build a house for the winter, and soon afterwards to collect a stock of provisions. They fell tree after tree, gnaw them into portable pieces and deposit these at the bottom of the lake close to the house. When the lake is frozen, they dive to the bottom to retrieve them. When the bark is stripped, they return the piece and pick up a new one. Their senses of hearing and smell are exquisitely fine. It requires the utmost precaution and vigilance of the hunter to steal within shot of them without detection and must always be done from the leeward. Their sense of sight is weak, and they seldom appear abroad during the day. On account of the value of its skin the beavers are the chief object of chase with the Indians. They are acquainted with the spots where these animals abound and hunt over these places alternately and periodically, allowing the beavers three years to regenerate. We shot many of them for provision.

Geese and ducks are met with in great numbers in the interior, the ducks in particular in the central parts of the island. There, remote from man, they breed undisturbed on the edges and islands of the ponds and lakes. The geese molt soon after their arrival in the spring; and owing to the loss of their pinion feathers, are unable to fly during the summer or breeding seasons, but they can then run faster than a man on the marshes. They feed on berries and the seed of grasses. They become enabled to fly in September. When the snow falls, they collect in flocks and fly off to the southern shores of the island and from thence to the Gulf of St. Lawrence. By December they take flight in immense flocks to the southern parts of America to return in the spring. The ducks are the last of the birds of passage seen here. Loon of two species breed in the interior, almost every lake being occupied during the summer season by a pair of them. Likewise, the common seagull early in the spring, which fly off to the sea in July and August.

The rivers and lakes abound with trout of three or four kinds, differing in size and colour. In one of the source branches of Gander River, which we crossed, we caught some small fish, apparently salmon fry, a species of fish, larger than the trout is said by the Indians to be found in several of the larger lakes.

We were nearly a month in passing over one savanna after another. In the interval there are several low granite beds, stretching as the savannas, northerly and southerly. During this time, we shot only a few deer, but many geese, ducks, and beavers, which, with trout, constituted our principal food. When we had no game to subsist on, the killing of which though certain was irregular, we subsisted on berries which some spots produced in prodigious abundance. I longed for bread for about ten days after our stock was consumed but after that did not miss it.

When we met deer in a herd, we seldom failed in shooting the fattest. The venison was excellent; the fat upon the haunches of some of them was two inches in thickness. We shot them with ball or swan shot, according to distance. The leading stag of a herd is generally the fattest, he is as tall as a horse and must sometimes be shot at full speed or sometimes by surprise. We saw a solitary stag rubbing his antlers against a larch tree on a plain, my Indian, treading lightly, approached him from behind and struck him on the head with an axe, but did not knock him down and the deer galloped off.

The flesh of the beaver is by the Indians esteemed the finest of all quadrupeds of the chase, and that of the young beaver justly so—in taste it is more like lamb. Beavers are commonly shot on the water; they seldom come out of their houses by day but are abroad all night. The black duck shot in the interior, remote from the sea, is the finest bird for the table in Newfoundland. The trout are so easily caught in the rivulets in the interior as to take the artificial fly, merely by holding out the line in the hand without a rod. No country in the world can afford finer sport than the interior of this island in the months of August and September. The beasts of the chase are of a large class, and the cover for all game excellent.

We occasionally crossed some of the large lakes on rafts, when our course lay across them and the wind happened to be fair, there appeared nothing to induce us to go round their extremities. We accomplished this by fastening together three or four trunks of trees with withes, held up a thick bush for a sail, and were blown over. There was, of course, considerable risk to our accoutrements attending this primitive mode of navigation.

The proportion of water to land in the savanna country is very great. In some directions northward one-half seems to be lakes, of every size and form; in other directions one-third and seldom less. The marbled, glossy surface as it appeared from the rising ground was singularly novel and picturesque.

In some of the forests, stripes of the trees are all borne down in the same direction flat to the earth by wind, and the havoc displayed is awful. Such parts were almost impassable. The way through the woods elsewhere except by the deer paths is obstructed by wind-fallen trees and brushwood. There are extensive districts remarkable for abundance of berries which attract great numbers of black bears. Although we have seen tracks of wolves every day and were sometimes within a few yards of them in the thickets, yet we only caught a glimpse of one of them. They lie in wait amongst the bushes and listen for the approach of deer and rush upon them. When they saw man instead of deer they immediately fled. There are two kinds of wolves here—one large, that prowls singly or in couples, another small, sometimes met with in packs.

In the whole of this savanna territory which forms the eastern central portion, there rises but one mountain which is a solitary peak of granite, standing very conspicuous about forty-five miles north from the mouth of the west Salmon River of Fortune Bay on the south coast. It served as an object by which to check our course and distance for about two weeks. I named it Mount Sylvester, the name of my Indian.

This province of savannas, of no territorial value at present, is destined to become a very important integral part of Newfoundland. Judging from their countless paths, and of the size and condition of the few deer we met it is already amply stocked with that kind of cattle of which no part of Northeast America possesses so peculiar a territory.

What superficial drainage and tilling might affect towards raising the green crops here remains to be proved.

Many of the savannas exhibit proofs of being once wooded; and in some places with a much larger growth of trees than that at present in their vicinity but are now partially or wholly covered with the results of savanna fires, originating with the Indians, and from lightening; and it would seem that a century or more must elapse in this climate before a forest of the same magnitude can be reproduced naturally on the savannas. It is observed of peat that burning and the turning of the surface by agricultural implements are the chief means by which the vegetation of these soils is exchanged for more profitable plants. To these must be added the growth of larch under which the original covering is gradually replaced by a green and grassy surface, applicable to the pastorage of cattle.

The fruit of the sarsaparilla, two kinds, were ripe in the beginning of October. Wild currants, gooseberries, and raspberries were plentiful in many places, the latter, as in all other parts of North America, only where the woods have been recently burnt. The berries here are much superior to the berries of the same species near the seacoast. They appear to grow for little immediate purpose as the quantity which the bears, foxes, and the birds fatten upon is comparatively inconsiderable to that produced.

Fogs are not frequent in the interior. There was not a foggy day until the fourth of October, which came with a southerly wind. There was no frost to hurt vegetation materially until the third of October, and that unaccompanied with snow. But the frost of that night changed one-half of the vegetation of the savannas from a light vegetable green to a yellow colour. Our attention was arrested twice by observing the tracks of a man on the savannas. After a scrupulous and minute examination, we concluded that one of them was that of a Mickmack or Mountaineer Indian, who had been hunting here in the preceding year. The other track was on the shores of Gower Lake, of an Indian who had passed by this season apparently from the Bay of Despair towards Gander Bay. We saw no traces, however, of the Red Indians.

October 7th. The nights and mornings were now frosty; and the vegetable kingdom had put on its autumnal colouring of various tints. The waters as well as the air were becoming chillier every day. A favourable change of wind did not now bring the accustomed mildness of temperature.

We have been occupied since eleventh September in travelling the savanna country. A hilly ridge in the westward, lying northerly and southerly, which had been in view several days, and about the centre of the Island, on our near approach bore an aspect different from any we had yet seen, appearing of a bright brown colour along the summit. The rocks for some miles to the eastward were often of various colours. On arriving on it this ridge proved to be a serpentine deposit, including a variety of rocks, all lying in nearly vertical strata alternating. The mineralogical appearances here were altogether so singular that I resolved to stop a day or two to examine them. All the highest parts of the ridge were formed of large angular blocks of quartz and were extremely sterile. The other rocks were noble serpentine, varying in colour from black, green, to yellow, and from translucent to semi-transparent. In strata nearly a yard wide—steatite, or soap stone and various other magnesian rocks. On sterile earthy patches lay heaps of loose fragments of asbestos, rock wood, rock cork, rock leather, rock horn, rock bone, and stones light in the hand resembling burnt pottery but evidently detached from adjoining strata and veins. I could not divest myself from the feeling that we were in the vicinity of a quiescent volcano.

The beaches of many of the lakes in the neighbourhood are formed of disintegrated fragments of those rocks. At one lake in particular which I in consequence denominated Serpentine Lake, the beauty and interesting appearance of some of the beaches, composed entirely of rolled fragments of these rocks of every kind and colour, the red, yellow, and green were prevailing. Serpentine Lake is comparatively small. It is known to the Mickmack Indian by the Indian name for it, or Stone Pipe Lake from their procuring here Verd antique, and other magnesian rocks, out of which they carve or chisel tobacco pipes, much prized by them.

In the woods on the margin of Serpentine Lake we found an old birch-bark canoe of the Mickmack Indians, the same as those used by those people at the seacoast. It had been brought up from the Bay of Despair at the south coast of the Island, by those of the Cod Roy River, which runs through this and intervening lakes. We inferred that the portages between Serpentine Lake and the seacoast were not very extensive or difficult. Here then is a route of the Indians by which the centre of the Island may be approached with the same canoe, and close by are the sources of rivers, that flow to the north coast.

There was an inhabited beaver's house at the south end of Serpentine Lake, and we shot three of the family that occupied it for food. There were also several herds of deer around. I designated this interesting district, which forms the centre nearly of Newfoundland, in honour of an excellent friend and distinguished promoter of science and enterprise, Professor Jameson, of Edinburgh—Jameson's Mountains. Judging from the rise in the land for about thirty miles to the eastward, they are about twelve hundred feet above the level of the sea. Future travellers may easily reach Jameson's Mountains by the route mentioned; and I hope some may soon follow the first there, for they deserve a much more perfect examination than could be given on a first visit by a half worn-out pedestrian traveller.

October 10th. Being now near the centre of the Island, upwards of one hundred and ten miles from the most inland part of Trinity Bay, about ninety miles of the distance being across the savannas—we had not yet seen a trace of the Red Indians. It had been supposed that all the central parts of the Island were occupied by these people, and I had been daily looking out for them.

It was now nearly five weeks that my Indian and I left the seacoast, and we were just half-way to St. George's Bay. We had for some time past felt severely the effects of continued excessive exertion of wet and of irregular supplies of food. My Indian, and only companion, complained much of the never-ending toil and would willingly have gone out to the sea, if I had yielded to his wish. But with me it was "now or never"; and I had apprehensions of being overtaken by the winter ere we could reach St. George's Bay. To keep my Indian at the toilsome task, I had sometimes to encourage him by promises of future reward, sometimes excite him by emulation by allusions to the fame of the Indian hunters for enduring fatigue and hardships beyond what the white man could bear and again picture the shame consequent on his leaving me in the country to perform alone what we had set out to do together.

Part V. Continue the Journey into the Western Interior.

In the west, mountain succeeds mountain in irregular succession, rugged and bleak. Encumbered with many additional mineralogical specimens, we took our departure from the interesting central mountains, for my part hoping that I might yet see them again. We were sometimes compelled to climb and creep our way over confused heaps of granite and white compact quartz. There are occasional marshes, and some of the less exposed spots produce stunted spruce and larch trees; other spots produce ground berries in great plenty. A species of Ledum or Indian tea is met with here, different from that commonly found at the seacoast. Deer now begin to appear in small herds in every direction.

October 11th. While surveying a large lake we decried a faint column of smoke issuing from amongst islands near the south shore, about five miles distant. The time we hoped had at last come to meet the Red Indians. The Red Indians had been reported not to frequent the south side of the Island. It was too late in the day to reconnoitre; and my Indian went in pursuit of a herd of deer in another direction, as we had no provisions for supper. At sunset he did not meet me at the appointed wood in a valley hard by, nor did he return by midnight, nor at all. I dared not exhibit a fire on the hill, as a beacon to him, in sight of the strange encampment. His gun might have burst and injured him, he might have fled, or been surprised by the party on the lake.

October 12th. At daybreak the atmosphere was frosty, and the slender white column of smoke still more distinctly seen. There were human beings there and, deserted, I felt an irresistible desire to approach my fellow creatures whether they should prove friendly or hostile. With no appearance of my Indian at noon, I left my knapsack and all encumbrances and descended through thickets and marshes towards the nearest part of the lake. The extent of the lake was uncertain, but it was apparent that it would require two days at least to walk round either end to the nearest point of the opposite shore to the occupied island. I therefore kept on my own side to discover who the party were. By firing off my gun, if the party were Red Indians, they would in all probability move quickly on hearing the report, and they having no firearms, my fire would not be answered. If they were other Indians, my fire would be returned. I fired. By and by the report of a strange gun travelled among the islands, and thus all my doubts and apprehensions were dispelled. The report of this gun was the first noise I had heard caused by man, except by my Indian and myself, for more than five weeks, and it excited very peculiar feelings.

In about an hour my lost Indian unexpectedly made his appearance from the direction where we had parted on the preceding evening. He accounted for himself, that after having shot a stag about two miles from the spot appointed for our encampment, he attempted to get round the west of the lake to reconnoitre the party on the island, but found the distance too great, and getting benighted, had slept in the woods.

Soon afterwards, to my great delight, there appeared among some woody islets in front, which precluded the view of the other side of the lake, a small canoe with a man seated in the stern, paddling softly towards us, with an air of serenity and independence possessed only by the Indian. After a brotherly salutation with me, and the two Indians kissing each other, the hunter proved to be unable to speak English or French. They, however, soon understood one another, for the stranger, although a mountaineer from Labrador, could speak a little of the Mickmack language, his wife being a Mickmack. The mountaineer tribe belongs to Labrador, and he told us that he had come to Newfoundland, hearing that it was a better hunting country than his own, and, that he was now on his way hunting from St. George's Bay to the Bay of Despair to spend the winter with the Indians there. He had left St. George's Bay two months before and expected to be at the Bay of Despair in two weeks hence.

This was his second year in Newfoundland; he was accompanied by his wife only. My Indian told him that I had come to see the rocks, the deer, the beavers, and the Red Indians and to tell King George what was going on in the middle of that country. He said St. George's Bay was about two weeks walk from us if we knew the best way and invited us over with him in his canoe to rest a day at his camp, where he said he had plenty of venison, which was readily agreed to on my part.

The island on which the mountaineer's camp was lay about three miles distant. The varying scenery as we paddled towards it, among innumerable islands and inlets, was beautiful. His canoe was similar to those described to have been used by the ancient Britons on the invasion by the Romans. It was made of wickerwork, covered over outside with deer skins sewed together and stretched on it, nearly of the usual form of canoes, with a bar or beam across the middle and one on each end to strengthen it. The skin covering, flesh side out, was fastened or laced to the gunwales, with thongs of the same material. Owing to decay and wear it requires to be renewed once in from six to twelve weeks. It is in these temporary barks that the Indians of Newfoundland of the present day navigate the lakes and rivers of the interior. They are easily carried, owing to their lightness, across the portages from one water to another, and when damaged easily repaired.

His wigwam was situated in the centre of a wooded islet, at which we arrived before sunset. The approach from the landing place was by a mossy carpeted avenue formed by the trees having been cut down in that direction for firewood. The sight of a fire, not of our own kindling, of which we were to partake, seemed hospitable. It was occupied by his wife seated on a deer skin busy sewing together skins of the same kind to renew the outside of the canoe we had just found, which required it. A large Newfoundland dog, her only companion in her husband's absence, had welcomed us at the landing place with signs of the greatest joy. Sylvan happiness reigned here.

His wigwam was of the semicircular form, covered with birch rind and dried deer skins, the fire on the fore ground outside. Abundance and neatness pervaded the encampment. On horizontal poles over the fire, hung quantities of venison stakes, being smoked dry. The hostess was cheerful, and a supper, the best the chase could furnish, was soon set before us on sheets of birch rind. They told me to "make their camp my own and use everything in it as such." Kindness so elegantly rendered by these people of nature in their solitude, commenced to soften those feelings which had been fortified against receiving any comfort except that of my own administering. The excellence of the venison, and of the flesh of young beavers, could not be surpassed. A cake of hard deer's fat with scraps of suet, toasted brown, intermixed was eaten with the meat; soup was the drink.

Our hostess after supper sang several Indian songs at my request. They were plaintive and sung in a high key. The song of a female and her contentment in this remote and secluded spot exhibited the strange diversity there is in human nature. My Indian entertained them incessantly until nearly daylight with stories about what he had seen in St. John's. Our toils were for the time forgotten.

The Mountaineer had occupied this camp for about two weeks, deer being very plentiful all around the lake. His larder, which was a kind of shed, erected on the rocky shore for the sake of a free circulation of air, was in reality a well-stocked butcher's stall, containing parts of a half-dozen fat deer, also the carcasses of beavers, of otters, of musk rats, and of marten, all methodically laid out. His property consisted of two guns and ammunition, an axe, some good culinary utensils of iron and tin, blankets, an apartment of dried deer skins to sleep on and with which to cover his wigwam—the latter with the hair off; a collection of skins to sell at the seacoast, consisting of those of beaver, otter, marten, musk rat and deer, the last dried and hair off; also a stock of dried venison in bundles. Animal flesh of every kind, in steaks, without salt, smoke-dried on the fire for forty-eight hours, becomes nearly as light and portable as cork, and will keep sound for years. It thus forms a good substitute for bread, and by being boiled two hours recovers most of its original qualities.

The Red Indians' country, or the waters which they frequented, we were told by the Mountaineer, lay six or seven miles to the north of us, but at this season of the year, these people were likely to be farther to the northward at the Great Lake of the Red Indians; also, that about two weeks before there was a party of Mickmack hunting at the next large lake to the westward, about two days walk from us, and that the deer were very plentiful to the westward. He also described the nature of the country and made drawings upon sheets of birch-rind of the lakes, rivers, mountains, and woods that lay in the best route to St. George's Harbour. This lake, called Meelpegh, or Crooked Lake, by the Indians, I also named in honour of Professor Jameson. It is nine or ten miles in length and joined by a strait to Burnt Bay Lake. It is one of the chains of lakes connected by the East Bay River of the Bay of Despair and running through Serpentine Lake which forms a part of the great route of the Indians.

October 14th. We left the veteran Mountaineer James John by name, much pleased with our having fallen in with him. He landed us from the canoe on the south shore of the lake, and we took our departure for the westward, along the south side. Truly could this man proclaim: "I'm monarch of all I survey, my right there is none to dispute; from the centre all round to the sea, I am lord of the fowl and the brute."

October 15th. There is a considerable quantity of fir woods on the borders of the lake. We fell in with a summer as well as a winter beavers' house, both inhabited, evidently by the same family, this being the time when they are changing their abodes. We found none of them at home. The first snow fell this afternoon with a gentle wind from the north-north-east, and so thick as to compel us to shelter and encamp in a wood that happened fortunately to be near. It continued to snow so heavy that at midnight our fire was extinguished, and firewood buried; but the silent uniform fall and pressure of the snow over our screen, and the blankets in which we were wrapped, kept us warm.

October 16th. In the morning three feet of snow covered the ground in the woods, and on the open ground it was deeper. Our provisions were exhausted, nor could we get through the snow to look for game. Weakened and miserable, we looked anxiously for a change of wind and thaw. At night a thaw came, but with it a southerly wind that brought both the snow and many of the largest trees to the ground together. Our fire was buried again and again by the snow from the trees, and as we were as likely to be killed while standing up as lying down, by the trees that crashed and shook the ground around us all night, we lay still wrapped in our blankets amidst the danger, and providentially escaped unhurt. I called the nearby hill Mount Misery.

October 17th. We were still storm-stayed and could only view the wreck of the forest close to us. Our situation was truly miserable; but the snow was fast melting away. I felt alarmed at the winter setting in thus early, for the consequences ere we could reach the seacoast.

October 18th. The snow having shrunk a foot at least, we left our wretched encampment and after a most laborious walk of six or eight miles through snow, thickets, and swollen brooks, and passing many deer, without however being able to get within shot of them we not only reached the lake to the westward, but to our great joy also discovered the encampment of the Indians of whom we had been told by the Mountaineer. The party were encamped in one large wigwam, or kind of hut. We entered with little ceremony, my Indian kissing them all—male and female. None of them could speak English, and only one of them a little French. A deer skin was spread for me to sit on, at the innermost part of the dwelling. My Indian interpreted and introduced me in the same particular terms as before.

They were Mickmacks and natives of Newfoundland and expressed themselves glad to see me in the middle of their country, as the first white man that had ever been here. The

Indian amongst his fellows is a purely self-dependent being—an innate power of self-denial raises him above dependence upon others and keeps him beyond their interference even in distressing wants, which yields mental triumph and glory. Want implies inability in the hunter. I observed these people bestow, and my Indian receive attention, with seeming indifference. He smoked the pipe given to him with the same composure as after a feast, although starvation and unconcealable hunger were depicted in his countenance.

Supper was soon ready, which consisted entirely of boiled venison. All seated around the fire, in the centre of the wigwam, partook at once—although, enfeebled by want of sustenance, I could eat only a few mouthfuls. The jaws would not perform their office without great pain from want of practice. Fortunately, the stomach sympathised, for it could bear but little. They told us that we might reach Saint George's Bay in about ten days; that they had left that place in the middle of summer, and had since then been hunting in the western interior, several weeks latterly having been spent at this lake, where deer were plenty; and that they intended in a few weeks hence, before the lakes and rivers were frozen over, to repair to White Bear Bay, to spend the winter, that place having been always celebrated for immense herds of deer passing by in the winter season. The Indian idea of a road is to Europeans little else than a probability of *reaching* a distant place *alive;* and I foresaw, from their report, much suffering before we could reach St. George's Bay.

Here were three families, amounting to thirteen persons in number. The men and boys wore surtouts made of deer skins, the hair outside, buttoned, and belted round them, which looked neat and comfortable. Their caps were of mixed fur; they had not procured much fur for sale, only a few dozen marten, some otter and musk rat skins; of beaver skins they had very few, as beavers are scarce in the western interior, it being too mountainous for woods, except on the sheltered borders of some of the lakes. In the woods around the margin of this lake the Indians had lines of path equal to eight or ten miles in extent, set with wooden traps, or dead falls, about one hundred yards apart, baited for martens, which they visited every second day. They had two skin canoes in which they paddled around the lake to visit their traps and bring home their game.

The Red Indian country we were told was about ten or fifteen miles northward of us, but that at this time, as the Mountaineer had likewise informed us, these people were all farther to the northward, at the Great Lake, where they were accustomed to lay up their winter stock of venison. These people corroborated previous as well as subsequent inquiries respecting the number of their own, and of the other communicating tribes in the Island.

Part VI. Of the Red Indians and the Other Tribes

All the Indians in the Island, exclusive of the Red Indians, amount to nearly a hundred and fifty, dispersed in bands, commonly at the following places or districts:—St. George's Harbour and Great Cod Roy River on the west coast; White Bear Bay, and the Bay of Despair on the south coast; Clode Sound in Bonavista Bay on the east; Gander Bay on the north coast; and occasionally at Bonne Bay and the Bay of Islands on the north-west coast. They are composed of Mickmack, joined by some of the Mountaineer tribe from Labrador, and a few of the Abenakis from Canada. The Esquimaux, from Labrador, occasionally, but seldom, visit the Island. There are twenty-seven or twenty-eight families altogether, averaging five to each family, and five or six single men. They all follow the same mode of life—hunting in the interior, from the middle of summer till the beginning of winter in single families, or in two or three families together. They go from lake to lake, hunting all over the country, around one before they proceed to the next. They paddle along the borders, and the men proceed on foot up every rivulet, brook, and rill, beavers being their primary object of search, otters, martens, musk-rats, and every living thing; secondly, when the lakes are connected by rivers, or when the portages between them are short, they proceed in or carry their canoes with them, otherwise they leave these, and build others on arriving on their destination.

The hunting season, which is the months of September and October, being over, they repair to the sea coast with their furs, and barter them for ammunition, clothing, tea, rum, etc. and then most of them retire to spend the winter at or near the mouths of the large rivers, where eels are to be procured through the ice by spearing, endeavouring at the same time to gain access to the winter paths of the deer.

A great division of the interior of Newfoundland is exclusively possessed and hunted over by Red Indians, and is considered their territory by the others. In former times, when the several tribes were upon an equality in respect of weapons, the Red Indians were considered invincible and frequently waged war upon the rest, until the latter got fire-arms put into their hands by Europeans. The Red Indians are even feared yet, and described as very large athletic men. They occupy the Great or Red Indian Lake, and many other lakes in the northern part of the Island, as well as the great River Exploits. Along the banks of this river, and at the Great Lake, they are said to have extensive fences or pounds, by which they ensnare deer, and thus procure regularly in every fall a supply of venison for winter provisions.

Two of the Indians here had several times fallen in with the Red Indians, and on one occasion obtained possession of their camp, in which they assert they found some European blankets and other articles of clothing, which it is presumed they must have pilfered. They also stated that the Red Indians use the same kind of skin canoes in the interior as they themselves do, and that they paint themselves all over.

The tribes exclusive of the Red Indians have no chief in Newfoundland, but there are several individuals at St. George's Bay to whom they all pay deference. The Mickmack, although most of them born on this Island, consider Cape Breton, where the chiefs reside, as their head-quarters. Their several tribes intermarry. These people might be rendered useful if some of the leaders were noticed by the British Government. Had this been earlier done it might have saved that tarnish on humanity, the butchery of the interesting aborigines, the Red Indians, by Englishmen. The communicating tribes consume their share of British manufactures, and mainly contribute to the support of the fur trade of the Island. The French have their principal confidence and affection.

The Indians find their way through the forests by marks with which they are familiar. Thus, moss grows on the north and not on the south side of the trees; the tops and branches of trees have an inclination for stretching to the south-east; wind-fallen trees point to the northward, etc. They have a call or toll for every kind of beast and bird to bring them within shot—for the deer an outward snort, to imitate the stag; for the beaver a hiss, for the otter a whistle, etc.

They are Roman Catholics, but their religious ceremonies, of which they are observant, consist of a combination of that church and their own ceremonies blended together. The people of the camp, by the earliest dawn of day, all joined in prayer; and nearly the whole of a Sunday, on which it happened I was with them, they spent in singing hymns. They had in their possession a French manuscript of sacred music, given to them by the French Roman Catholic clergyman at the Island of St. Peter's, whom they consider their confessor, and endeavour to see once in two years.

The Indians seldom carry salt with them into the interior, nor with very few exceptions, do they require it. The Red Indians are, of course, unacquainted with salt, as well as with all foreign luxuries; when their food is altogether animal salt is not desired, nor does it seem to be necessary. Supper is the chief repast with the hunter; in the evening he enjoys the fruits of the day's chase, and recounts, in his turn, his adventures. Most of the Indians, when they would otherwise be in the prime of life, have broken constitutions by over-exertions, casualties, and exposure to weather. Their perilous mode of life also leads them to be more subject to some kinds of bodily infirmities than men in more dense societies. They know most of the remedies they need and collect them in nature. The roots of the following plants, among others, are used medicinally by them; *Geum rivale, Saracenia purpurea, Havernaria dilatate, Smilacrina borealis, Mergantnes trifolia, Salix vulgare,* and others.

October 21st. The weather having been mild for the last few days, much of the snow had dissolved, it lay chiefly on banks. The Indians put us across the lake, and we took our departure for the westward, refreshed by our two days' stay with them. The country now became mountainous, and almost destitute of wood, deer became more numerous, berries were very plentiful, and mostly in high perfection, although the snow had lately covered them. Indeed, the partridge berries were improved, and many spots were literally red with them.

October 22nd. On our march to-day we discovered a black bear feeding on berries on a hill about a mile off, and stole upon him unawares by a circuitous route from the leeward. We fired a shot each at him, both of which had effect; but he ran a mile before he fell. He was very fat, weighing about three hundred and fifty pounds. The fat round his body was four inches in some parts. We rested two days to feast on him, leaving the remainder, except what we could conveniently carry, with regret, from a lively apprehension of the future want of it. Bear's flesh is by many of the Indians esteemed next to that of beavers, and it has the peculiar quality of not clogging the stomach, however much of it is eaten. My Indian apprised me of this circumstance before hand, and availed himself of the fact, for on the night of the death of bruin, after we had both began, as I thought, to sleep, about two o'clock am, I found him busy roasting, frying, and devouring as voraciously as if he had eaten no supper.

October 24th. The winter had now fairly set in, the ponds were all frozen over, the birds of passage had deserted the interior for the sea coast, and the grouse had on their white winter coats; many hardships now awaited the traveller.

Part VII. General Features of the Western Interior, etc.

October 27th. The western territory is entirely primitive. No rocks appear but granite. The only soil is peat, which varies in quality according to situation. In the valleys some patches are very similar to the savanna peat in the eastward, but as the peat ascends, it becomes shallower and lighter until it terminates at the summit of the mountains in a mere matting. Lichen occupies the highest resting places for vegetation on the mountain tops. The trees, all vegetating upon peat, are often forced to assume new features. Particularly the larch creeps along the ground to leeward, where neither the birch nor spruce can exist. There are here the remains of extensive forests, destroyed by fire, where now there is not a tree within many miles. Neither reptile nor serpent of any kind had yet fallen under our notice, nor had the Indians ever seen or heard of any noxious animal being in the Island. It may therefore be concluded that there are none of this class here, common on the neighbouring islands and the continent.

Were the agriculturists of the coast to come here, they would see herds of cattle, fat on natural produce of the country, sufficient for the supply of provision to the fisheries, and the same animal fit, with a little training, to draw sledges at the rate of twenty miles an hour. Nature has liberally stocked Newfoundland with herds, finer than those Norway and Lapland can boast. These natural herds are the best adapted for this climate and pasture; and it is evident on witnessing their numbers, that all that is required to render the interior, now in waste, at once a well-stocked grazing country, through the means of employing qualified herdsmen, who would make themselves familiar with these herds and accompany them from pasture to pasture, as is done in Norway and Lapland with the reindeer there. When taken young these deer become very domestic and tractable. Were the intelligent resident inhabitants of the coast, who have an interest in advancing the country internally, to adopt a plan for effecting this object, under their own vigilance, benefits and comforts now unthought of could be realized. Norwegians or Lapland Finns could be easily introduced into the interior, if the Indians were unwilling or unfit.

We met many thousands of the deer, all hastening to the eastward, on their periodical migration. They had been dispersed since the spring on the mountains and barren tracts, in the west and north-west division of the interior, to bring forth and rear their young amidst the profusion of lichen and mountain herbage, and where they were, comparatively with the low lands, free from the persecution of flies. When the first frosts, as now in October, nip vegetation, the deer immediately turn towards the south and east, and the first fall of snow quickens their pace in those directions, as we now met them, towards the low grounds where browse is to be got and the snow not so deep over the lichens. In travelling herd follows herd in rapid succession over the whole surface of the country, all bending their course in the same way in parallel lines. The herds consist of from twenty to two hundred each, connected by stragglers or piquettes, the animals following each other in single files, a few yards or feet apart, as their paths show; were they in close bodies, they could not graze freely.

They continue to travel south-eastward until February or March, by which time the returning sun has power to soften the snow and permit of their scraping it off to obtain lichens underneath. They then turn round to the west, and in April are again on the rocky barrens and mountains where their favourite mossy food abounds the most and where in June, they bring forth their young. In October the frosty warning to travel returns. They generally follow the same routes year after year, but these sometimes vary, owing to irregularities in the seasons and interruptions by the Indians. Such are, in a general view, the curses and causes of the migrations of the deer, and these seem to be the chief design of animated nature in this portion of the earth. Lakes and mountains intervening cause the lines of the migration paths to deviate from the parallel; and at the necks of land that separate large lakes, at the extremity of lakes, the deer unavoidably concentrate in travelling. At those passes the Indians encamp in parties and stay for considerable intervals of time because they can there procure the deer with comparatively little trouble.

After the first great fall of snow, although the acclivities had been for a few days laid bare by the mild weather, the snow lay in banks in the valleys. Light snow-showers afterwards occasionally fell. We suffered much at night from the inclemency of the weather. The trees were here so stunted and scanty that we could hardly collect enough of brushwood and roots to keep a very small fire alive, and then we were unavoidably exposed. At one time, for three nights in succession, we could not find a dry spot of ground to lie upon. In such situations the want of sleep attended the want of shelter, and it was a contest between frost and fire which should have the supremacy over our bodies. Although we could shoot deer at intervals every day, no supply of food was adequate to support the system under the exhaustion and load of painful fatigue which we had to undergo. For my part I could measure my strength—that it would not obey the will and drag along the frame beyond two weeks more. Still, it was cheering to hope that that space of time would carry us to the west coast.

Ever since we left the last party of Indians, my Indian disputed with me about the course we should pursue, he obstinately insisting upon going to the southward. Perhaps he had a secret desire not to pass too near the Red Indian country, or he may have heard that some of his tribes were encamped in the direction he was inclined to go. As a separation might have led to serious consequences, I submitted from necessity.

October 28th. The small lakes were sufficiently frozen

over for us to walk upon them. As we advanced westward the aspect of the country became more dreary, and the primitive features more boldly marked. As we neared the south end of an extensive lake in order to get round it, we observed a low islet near the middle entirely covered with a large species of gull. Those birds seemed as if they had congregated to take flight before the lake was frozen over. At the extreme south end, we had to ford a rapid river of considerable size, running to the southward, which from its position, we inferred was "Little River," which discharges at the south coast.

October 29th. Drawing near to a mountain-ridge higher than any we had yet crossed, and which from appearance we supposed might be the last between us and the sea coast, we had great satisfaction in discovering smoke rising from a wood on the opposite side of a lake near the foot of it. We indulged in the hope that some timber party from the settlements at St. George's Bay was encamped here. Our toils were in fancy ended. On reaching the lake, the party encamped seemed to distrust us, not venturing to show themselves openly on the shore. After a time, however, they were convinced by our appearance, gestures, and the report of our guns, that we were neither Red Indians nor enemies. A canoe was launched and came across to us. The canoe was of the kind already described, of wicker-work, covered with skins, and paddled by two pretty Indian girls. I unceremoniously saluted them in the Indian manner and we accompanied them to their camp.

They were a party of Mickmack Indians, encamped at this lake because deer and firewood were plentiful. One man only belonged to this encampment, and he was out hunting when we arrived. They told us, to our no little mortification, that we were yet sixty miles from St. George's Harbour, or about five days walk if the weather should happen to be favourable, and that it lay in a north-west direction. The last information proved that my Indian had of late pertinaciously insisted on a wrong course. This small party consisted of eight individuals— one man, four women, and three children. One an infant, was strapped or laced to its cradle, and placed upright against the side of a wigwam, as any piece of domestic furniture might be.

They had left St. George's Harbour three months before; since then, had been in the interior, and intended to spend the winter at Great Cod Roy River in St. George's Bay. As every hour was precious towards the final accomplishment of my object, I proposed to my Indian host to accompany me to St. George's Bay; my offer was agreed to, and a stipulation made to set off in two hours. In the absence of this Indian, who told me his name was Gabriel, his family—consisting as already observed of females and children were to provide for themselves. For this purpose, two guns and ammunition were left with them. One of the young women was a capital shot; during our halt with them she left the camp and shot a fat deer close by. Having partaken of the best piece of venison the interior could produce, together with smoked deer's tongue, we set off. Owing to our enfeebled condition, this man's vigour and strength were enviable.

October 30th. Rain, snow, and wind, in the early part of the day compelled us to stop and encamp. We shot a hare the first we had killed, it was white, except the tips of the ears and tip of the tail, which always remain black. The hare of Newfoundland is the Arctic hare. It sometimes weighs fourteen pounds and upwards. The grouse, during severe snow storms at night, allow the snow to drift over them, and thus covered, obtain shelter. While in this situation a silver thaw sometimes comes on, and the incrustation on the surface becomes too thick for them to break through in the morning, and immense numbers of them perish by being in that manner enclosed.

When we were crossing a lake on the ice my Indian fell through and with great exertion saved himself. While he was struggling my new friend Gabriel stood still and laughed; Joe did not look for assistance, nor did the other evince the least disposition to render any, although he was, compared with my position on the lake, near to him. Upon my remonstrating with Gabriel about his manifesting a want of feeling towards Joe, when perishing, Joe himself replied to me, "Master, it is all right; Indian rather die than live owing his life to another." The other had acted in sympathy with the self-dependent sentiment of the Indians.

October 31st. We travelled over hills and across lakes about twenty miles, fording in that space two rivers running north-easterly, and which are the main source branches of the river Exploits. This large river has therefore a course of upwards of two hundred miles in one direction, taking its rise in the south-west angle of the Island and discharging at the north-east part. The Indians are all excellent shots, and the two men now with me displayed admirable skill in killing the deer at great distances and at full speed, with a single ball. Nearly a foot of snow had recently fallen, which cast a monotonous sublimity over the whole country, and in a great measure concealed the characteristics of the vegetable as well as the mineral kingdoms.

We encamped at night at the southern extremity of what is said by my Indian to be the most southern lake of the interior frequented by the Red Indians and through which flows the main source branch of the River Exploits. At the same lake, the Mickmack and the Indians friendly with them commence and terminate their water excursions from and to the west coast. They here construct their first skin canoes upon entering the interior, or leave their old ones upon setting off on foot for the sea coast. The distance to St. George's Harbour is twenty-five miles or upwards, which part of the journey must be performed on foot, because no waters of any magnitude intervene. I named the lake in honour of His Majesty George the IV.

November 1st. For nearly twenty miles to the westward of George the Fourth's Lake, the country is very bare, there being scarcely a thicket of wood. During the day we forded two rapid rivulets running south-west to St. George's Bay. Deer had hitherto passed us in innumerable straggling herds, but westward of George the Fourth Lake, and particularly as we neared the coast, very few were to be seen. While ascending a mountain, I felt myself suddenly overcome with a kind of delirium, arising I supposed from exhaustion and excessive exertion. But I fancied myself stronger than I was ever in my life. It is probable under that influence, that if the Indian who last joined us had not been present, I would have had a rencontre with my other Indian.

Part VIII. The West Coast

Continued November 1st. In the evening, about eighteen miles west of George the Fourth's Lake, from the summit of a snowy ridge which defines the west coast, we were rejoiced to get a view of the expansive ocean and St. George's Harbour. Had this prospect burst upon us in the same manner a month earlier, it would have created in my mind a thousand pleasures, the impression of which I was now too callous to receive; all was now however accomplished, and I hailed the glance of the sea as home. There was scarcely any snow to be seen within several miles of the seacoast, while the mountain range upon which we stood, and the interior in the rear, were covered.

The descent was now very precipitous and craggy. A rapid river called Flat Bay River across which we were to ford, or if swollen, to pass over upon a raft, flowed at the foot of the ridge. It threatened rain, and the sun was setting; but the sight of the sea urged us onward. By sliding down rill courses, and traversing the steeps, we found ourselves with whole bones, but many bruises, at the bottom, by one o'clock on the following morning. We then, by means of carrying a large stone each on our backs in order to press our feet against the bottom, and steadying ourselves by placing one end of a pole, as with a staff or walking-stick, firmly upon the bottom on the lee side to prevent the current from sweeping us away, step after step, succeeded in fording the river, and encamped by a good fire, but supperless, in the forest on the banks of the river.

November 2nd. In the afternoon we reached St. George's Harbour. The first houses we reached, two in number, close to the shore, belonged to Indians. They were nailed up, the owners not having yet returned from the interior after their fall's hunting. The houses of the European residents lay on the west side of the harbour, which is here about a mile wide, and near the entrance; but a westerly gale of wind prevented any intercourse across. Having had no food for nearly two days, we ventured to break open the door of one of the houses— the captain or chief's as we understand from my last Indian, and found what we wanted—provisions and cooking utensils. The winter stock of provisions of this provident man named Emanuel Gontgont, the whole having been provided at the proper season, consisted of six barrels of pickled fish, of different kinds, vis. young halibuts and eels, besides dried cod fish, seal oil in bladders, and two barrels of maize or Indian corn flour.

November 3rd. We were still storm-stayed in the Indian house, in the midst of plenty. It seemed remarkable that the provisions were entirely free from the ravages of rats and other vermin, although left without any precaution to guard against such. There was a potato and turnip field close to the house, with the crops still in the ground, of which we availed ourselves, although now partly injured by frost.

November 4th. A party of Indians arrived from the interior, male and female, each carrying a load of furs. Our landlord was amongst them. Instead of appearing to notice with displeasure his door broken open and the house occupied by strangers, he merely said upon looking round and my offering an explanation, "Suppose me here you take all these things."

We crossed the harbour, and were received by the residents—Jersey and English, and their descendants—with open arms. All European and other vessels had left this coast a month before, so that there was no chance of my obtaining a passage to St. John's, or to another country. There were too many risks attending the sending to sea any of the vessels here at this season, although I offered a considerable sum to the owners of any of them that would convey me to Fortune Bay on the south coast, from whence I might obtain a passage to Europe by some of the ships that had probably not yet sailed from the mercantile establishments there.

After a few days I parted with my Indians—the one, who had with painful constancy accompanied me across the Island, joining his countrymen here to spend the winter with them, and return to his friends at the Bay of Despair in the following spring; the other, having renewed his stock of ammunition and other outfits, returning to his family which we had left in the interior.

Having now crossed the Island, I cannot help thinking that my success was in part owing to the smallness of my party. Many together could not so easily have sustained themselves; they would have multiplied the chances of casualties, and thereby of the requisition of the attendance, and detention of the able. It is difficult to give an idea of, or to form an estimate equivalent to, the road-distance gone over. The toil and deprivation were such that hired men, or followers of any class, would not have endured them.

I remained at St. George's Bay Harbour under the hospitable roof of Mr. Philip Messervey, the principal inhabitant, to rest and recover from the fatigues and deprivations of my journey, and from a hurt received while descending the mountains to the coast.

At St. George's Harbour there are about twenty families, amounting to one hundred souls, most of their parents being natives of England and Jersey. Their chief occupation is salmon fishing and furring; a little cod fish is also cured. They catch annually three or four hundred barrels of salmon, according to the success of the fishery, and procure fur, including what is obtained from the Indians by barter, to the value of nearly four hundred pounds. They possess four schooners, three of them being built by themselves and one by the Indians, in which most of the male inhabitants make one voyage annually, either to Halifax, Nova Scotia, or to St. John's, Newfoundland, to dispose of their fish and fur. Some of them barter their produce with trading vessels from Canada and New Brunswick, or with the vessels of any other country that may come to the coast, receiving provisions and West Indian produce in exchange. They all cultivate potatoes, and some keep a few cows. Along the banks of the several rivers which flow into the harbour are strips of good land; some good pine spars, and birch timber fit for shipbuilding are also to be found there. St. George's Harbour, although barred, may be entered by vessels of any burthen. There is no other ship harbour between Cape Ray and Port au Port, but there is good anchorage in the roadstead between Cod Roy Island and the main island near Cape Anguille. None of the other harbours can be entered even by small craft when the wind blows strong westwardly.

Taking an aggregate view of the French Shore, there are resident upon it upwards of fifty British families consisting of about three hundred souls, who catch annually nearly seven hundred barrels of salmon; fur, to the value of six hundred pounds; cod fish and herrings, four hundred pounds; making, together with the shipping built, the total value of the exports of the British residents on the French Shore, 2,400 pound or 2,500-pound sterling. The usual mode of paying servants on the west coast is allowing them one-third of the fruits of their industry, salmon, fur or otherwise, the employer providing diet. The principle is well worthy of imitation on the east coast. St. George's Harbour, locally called Flat Bay, as well as the estuaries of all the rivers on the west coast, is famous for an abundance of eels. The Indians take them in great quantities by spearing them in the mud, and pickle them for winter use. If there was a market, they might be, as indeed they have been to a limited extent, exported. The French Shore of Newfoundland is one of the most valuable in the globe for fisheries. At this day it is nearly in a primitive state, although in summer occupied by hundreds of French ships, which send forth their thousands of batteaux and men brought from France, all eager in the pursuit of the cod fishery. Mackerel might be taken at St. George's Bay in any quantity in the fall of the year only, but none are caught now.

This fishery, were it pursued, would succeed that of the salmon in the order of season and the process of curing is similar. Herrings might likewise be caught to supply and suit any demand and market, as they are of all sizes. Whale and seal also abound in their respective seasons, but none are killed. The British residents on the French Shore feel very insecure in the enjoyment of their salmon fishery and in any extension of their property, by reason of the peculiar tenure in regard to the French. A satisfactory solution of the mystery as to their rights has not yet been communicated to them, although they have made repeated applications at head quarters at St. John's. But the French are at present friendly disposed to them, although their rights are treated as mere sufferance. There is here neither clergyman, school-master, church nor chapel. Yet during my short stay, there was one wedding (an Indian couple, Roman Catholics, married by a Protestant resident, reading the Church of England service from a French translation) and four christenings, celebrated by the same person, with feasts and rejoicings suitable to such events.

November 16th. Being now much recovered by the various attentions at St. George's Harbour, during my stay of ten days, I set out on foot to the southward along the sea shore, accompanied by two of the young Jersey residents, in hopes, by walking and boating to reach Fortune Bay, a distance of upwards of two hundred miles, before all the vessels for the season had sailed for Europe. We slept as intended, in a deserted salmon fisher's hut on the shore, being unable to reach any habitation.

November 17th. We forded the mouths of several minor streams, and that of the north of third Barasway River, it having no harbour at its estuary. In the evening reached the second Barasway River, a distance of twenty-four miles from St. George's Harbour, and where reside the nearest inhabitants. Our walk all the way was on a sandy rocky beach at the bottom of cliffs, washed by the sea. The cliffs are formed chiefly of red sand-stone, red ochre, blue clay, and gypsum, sixty or seventy feet and upwards in height, with a deep bed of red alluvial earth everywhere superimposed.

In the immediate vicinity of the Barasway Rivers, as well as elsewhere in St. George's Bay, there are both sulphurous and saline springs. Coal of excellent quality lies exposed in strata in the bed and banks of a rivulet between the first and second Barasway Rivers, about seven and nine miles from its mouth. The inhabitants at the Barasway Rivers were now in their winter houses under the shelter of the woods, having recently left their summer residences at the shore. Like the people at St. George's Harbour, they are industrious and frugal. The following animals are entrapped and shot here for their furs: Martens, foxes, otters, beavers, musk rats, bears, wolves, and hares. Although ermines are numerous, the inhabitants do not preserve their skins, because they are small, their value not being known. Some of the residents have well-stocked farms, the soil being good. Oats, barley, potatoes, hay etc. are produced to perfection and even wheat. As evidence of the capabilities of portions of Newfoundland for agricultural purposes, notice must be taken of the farm of my hostess, Mrs. Hulan, at the second Barasway River. The stock on it consisted of six milch cows, besides other cattle; the dairy could not be surpassed in neatness and cleanliness, and the butter and cheese were excellent; the butter made, exclusive of what was kept for her comparatively numerous domestic establishment was sold, part to the residents at other places in the bay, and part to trading vessels that come to the coast in summer. The cellar was full of potatoes and other vegetables for winter use. She was also an experimental farmer, and exhibited eight different kinds of potatoes, all possessing different qualities to recommend them. Of domestic poultry there was an ample stock. Mrs. Hulan, although not a native, had lived in St. George's Bay upwards of sixty years, and remembers the celebrated navigator, Cook, when he surveyed the coast. She is indefatigably industrious and useful, and immediately or remotely related to, or connected with, the whole population of the bay, over whom she commands a remarkable degree of maternal influence and respect.

The coast southward from hence to Cod Roy, a distance of upwards of thirty miles, and where the nearest inhabitants in that direction were, was too rugged and bold to admit of our walking along the shore. The inhabitants here, or at St. George's Harbour, were ready to exert themselves to get me forward. A forced march, which might occupy ten days, over a snow-covered mountainous country in the rear of the coast, has few attractions just now, and on November 19th, the weather proving favourable, two young men of Mrs. Hulan's establishment launched forth with me in a small skiff to row and sail close along the shore, as wind and weather might permit. My kind hostess, aware of the probable detention we might meet, provisioned the little bark for two days.

November 20th, 21st, and 22nd. While passing in a boat, the formation of the coast could only be viewed, not examined. Between the south Barasway River and Cod Roy the coast is a continued range of cliffs, along which there is neither harbour nor shelter of any kind for even a boat. A light skiff or punt is there the safest mode of conveyance along this horrific coast in the inclement season of the year; for here and there between the cliffs there is a spot of beach with a ravine well known to the inhabitants, at which, although far apart in the event of being overtaken by bad weather, a skiff can run ashore, and the crew at the same instant jumping out, haul her up beyond the reach of the surf. This we were forced to do several times, and to clamber to the top of the cliffs until the weather moderated.

November 23rd. We doubled Cape Anguille and reached Cod Roy. Cape Anguille seems to be formed of quartz rock in front and granite in the rear, it being a projection of the granitic ridge that defines the west coast. Cod Roy—and here there is an island of the same name—is close to Cape Anguille on the south. The inhabitants, as at the Barasway Rivers, were in their winter houses in the woods, and their boats laid up for the winter. I, however, soon obtained a volunteer in the principal resident, named Parsons, to convey me as soon as the weather would permit in his skiff round Cape Ray, and to the next place where a boat could be procured. Owing to the shelter and anchorage for shipping at Cod Roy, as already noticed, and to its immediate proximity to the fine fishing grounds about Cape Ray, it is the central point of the French fisheries in summer. Many square-rigged vessels are here loaded with dried cod fish for France; and hundreds of batteaux brought from France in the fishing ships scatter from hence in all directions over the fishing grounds. There are here five resident families.

November 28th. Having waited at Cod Roy five days in vain for an abatement of the strong north-west wind to permit of our putting to sea in a skiff, I set out with Parsons on foot to the southward by the sea shore. Great Cod Roy River is about six miles south of Cod Roy Island. We crossed the gut or entrance between the sea and the expansive shallow estuary of the river in a boat of one of the residents. The entrance is barred with sand and has only about six feet of water. There reside here five families with their servants, amounting to twenty-eight souls. They catch about 40 barrels of salmon annually, which, with herring, and a trifling of cod fishery, are their chief means of subsistence. Coal is found on the south bank of the Great Cod Roy River, six or seven miles from the sea.

There were at this time ten Indian families encamped for the winter on the banks of Great Cod Roy River, about ten miles from its mouth. The chief attraction for the Indians here is the abundance of eels and trout. Little Cod Roy River is about six miles south of that of Great Cod Roy, and has also a gut at its estuary, which we in the like manner crossed in a boat. This estuary forms an expansive harbour inside. There are here two resident families only, amounting, with servants, to seventeen souls. They exist by furring, and a small cod fishery, the quantity of salmon caught being very trifling. The residents of Cod Roy and at these rivers, with the exception of Parsons, and one or two others recently settled there for the sake of the cod fishery, are extremely indolent and ignorant, differing in these respects from the rest of the inhabitants of St. George's Bay.

The soil in St. George's Bay is the best, and at the same time forms the most extensive tract of good soil anywhere on the coast of Newfoundland. It seldom exceeds two miles in breadth except at the rivers, and there it extends many miles up the country along the banks. Coal is reported to exist at other places on this coast, besides being at the Barasway and Cod Roy Rivers. The Indians say it lies exposed in such abundance on the surface of the earth near the mouth of a brook on the west side of Port au Port that they have made fires of it on the spot; and this is an excellent harbour for shipping. Verde antique, of a dark green colour, spotted or mottled with white, is found at the north of Port au Port on the bed of what is called the Coal River, a few miles from the sea, and brought down in pieces by the Indians for the manufacture of tobacco pipes. The natural productions of the west coast, viewed in relation to the neighbouring countries are well deserving the attention of Canada in particular.

November 29th. Cape Ray. Having slept the previous night in the winter house of one of the families at Little Cod Roy River, we walked to-day round Cape Ray, here leaving the French Shore and entering upon American Newfoundland, or that division of the coast on which the Americans have a right of fishing and of drying their fish. On the shore north of Cape Ray lay several wrecks of ships and their cargoes of timber. Cape Ray is a low point formed of dusky coloured traprock intersected in some places with vertical strata of green trap, running in an east and west direction. The coal formation of St. George's Bay adjoins. On the very Cape there resides during summer a person of the name of Wm. Windsor, with his family. We found him in his winter hut in a spruce wood two or three miles to the eastward of the Cape. The most perfect contentment, cheerfulness, poverty, and hospitality were the characteristics of the monarch of Cape Ray. His resources, through the means of fishing, enabled him to procure a sufficiency of coarse biscuit, molasses, and tea, by which, together with fowling, he supported his family.

The high lands of Cape Ray lie several miles inland, north-east of the Cape, and consist of a group of granite mountains seemingly nearly two thousand feet in height. The scenery among them is sublime. The vicinity of Cape Ray is remarkable for great numbers of foxes, induced here by the abundance of their chief food, viz, the partridge berry and hurtle berry. We were several days storm-stayed by winds and snow, and the inefficiency of the ice to bear us across the rivulets, at a boat harbour called the Barasway, six or seven miles east of the Cape. The person in whose winter house we stopped here, his summer residence being at Port au Basque at the eastward, had now entrapped and shot about eighty foxes, black, silver, grey, patch, and red, in less than two months; all those colours are produced at one litter. The foxes are mostly caught in iron spring-traps, artfully concealed in the pathways along the seashore.

Part IX. American Portion of Newfoundland

December 5th. Port au Basque, the nearest harbour to Cape Ray on the East, about twelve miles distant therefrom, we reached by boat from the Barasway. It had a fine open entrance, and good anchorage, and is sufficiently capacious for any number of ships to ride in safety. Four families reside here during the summer pursuing the cod fishery at that season, and the furring in winter. A small safe basin called Little Bay, with a narrow entrance, adjoins Port au Basque immediately on the East. There are no summer residences here, but two persons engaged in the cod fishery at the Dead Islands in summer were encamped in the woods for the winter. They undertook to convey me in their little skiff to Dead Island, the next harbour to the east; and in consequence, I here parted with my faithful and daring attendant, Parsons, from Cod Roy.

December 7th. Dead Island. Reached this place from Little Bay. The harbour, here called Pass, is fit for any ships, and is a narrow passage between a string of Islands and the main Island. Port au Basque and Channel and the Dead Island or Pass are both excellent stations at which to carry on the American fisheries. The fishing grounds in the vicinity of Cape Ray are probably the best on the Newfoundland coast for the resort of fishermen from a distance, they being peculiar in this important point, that the cod are always to be found in abundance upon them and caught at all seasons when the weather is not too boisterous, and then the neighbouring harbours mentioned afford shelter to the fishing craft. The fishery here may be commenced six weeks or a month earlier than at any other part of the coast and continued in the fall of the year until Christmas. Many industrious fishermen within a hundred miles eastward do not leave these grounds until the end of December.

The cod caught in October, November, and December is called winter fish. At Fortune Bay to the eastward, on the same coast, winter fish is caught by means of the smaller boats in the months of January, February, and March, in deep water close to the shores. The winter-caught fish is of a better quality than that taken at any other season. It is allowed to remain in dry salt during the winter and dried in the first warm weather in spring; being then sent to a foreign market, it arrives at an early season of the year when there is no other newly cured fish to compete, and brings fifty per cent or upwards more than the fish dried in the preceding year. There is no winter fish caught at Newfoundland except at the south-west coast.

At the Dead Islands three families reside in summer, whose chief pursuit is the cod fishery. I was here fortunate in finding a very respectable industrious inhabitant, named Thomas Harvey, still occupying his summer house at the shore, and his fishing boat or shallop not yet dismantled for the winter. Although no ordinary remuneration was equivalent to the risk at this inclement season on so dangerous a coast, Harvey unhesitatingly manned and provisioned his boat to enable me to reach Fortune Bay. It would have been impossible without the probability of being either frozen or starved to walk along this coast at this season of the year, it is so indented with deep bays and rivers, and in a manner uninhabited and unexplored.

December 8th. We set sail from the Dead Islands, passed by a harbour called Burnt Island, where two families reside who pursue the cod fishery. The weather being stormy, we were forced afterwards to put into the Seal Island, some fifteen miles to the eastward. Seal Island is a fine safe harbour with two entrances, one east, another west. There is only one resident family here, seemingly in good circumstances by means of the cod fishery. The prevailing rock here is mica slate.

December 11th. Strong winds and snow had compelled us to remain all night at Seal Island. We now got under way, with a fair wind, cheerfully passing by Harbour le Cou, uninhabited; Garia, with one resident family in summer; Indian Island, with one resident family; La Poile, a noble deep bay with two resident families; and reached Grand Brit, a good little harbour with two entrances, the west being the better, and where reside two families in summer, whose habitations were now locked up and deserted.

December 12th. Set sail and reached Cingserf, a good harbour for vessels of any size; the best anchorage is on the east side. It has no summer residents, nor could we discover any signs of winter occupants. Trap rock prevails here.

December 13th. Having passed the night at Cingserf, we set off again with a fair wind; touch at and pass through amongst the Burgeo Islands. Here is a sheltered roadstead with good anchorage. At Burgeo Islands there are eleven or twelve, and in the vicinity, five or six resident families. In the evening we reached the Rameo [Ramea] Islands, the east extremity of that portion of the Newfoundland coast at which the Americans have a right of fishing and of curing fish. There are only two resident families here.

The Americans have, by the treaty of Ghent, a right of fishing and curing their fish in common with British subjects, on the coast between Cape Ray and the Rameo Islands, an extent of about seventy-five miles. This portion of the coast, although possessing many fine harbours besides those noticed here, contain scarcely forty resident families, or two hundred and fifty souls on the whole of it. The chief pursuits of these people are the cod fishery in summer, and entrapping foxes and other wild animals for their skins in the fall. The salmon fishery is a very minor object, as the rivers are not so large nor numerous as on the west coast. The fishermen, or planters as they are called, obtain their outfits to enable them to carry on the fisheries from the merchants at Fortune Bay. They annually catch about three thousand cwts. or quintals or upwards of cod fish, make about forty-five tuns of cod oil, and obtain fur to the value of one hundred pounds.

The approach to many of the fine harbours here is dangerous from the want of surveys of the outer coast. Thousands of valuable lives have been lost by shipwreck, particularly to the eastwards of Cape Ray, in consequence of most dangerous currents and sunken rocks that exist there, being unnoticed upon any chart, and until the colonists themselves take up the cause of humanity, it is not likely these dangers will for a long time be made known or a light-house erected on the coast.

The residents here as at St. George's Bay, and at most of the north and west harbours of the Island, have both summer and winter houses. They retire to the residences or huts in the woods on the setting in of the winter, for facility of firewood and shelter; the labour attending the conveyance of fuel to their summer residences at the shore, which are exposed to every inclemency of the weather, being very great. They sometimes remove to a distance of thirty miles and even farther to the sequestered woods at the heads of bays and harbours, and on the banks of rivers, taking with them their boats, furniture, and provisions, and re-appear at the coast in the month of April. Sea fowl and birds of passage resort to the south-west coast in great numbers in the fall of the year; and during that season, as well as in winter, constitute a considerable portion of the provisions of the inhabitants.

The dogs here are admirably trained as retrievers in fowling and are otherwise useful. They are fed on fish, purposely cured for them. The lynx, a common animal in all the adjacent countries, is not considered to be a native of Newfoundland. Neither squirrel, porcupine, or racoon have been met with on the Island. Penguins were once numerous at this coast, their breeding place having been the Penguin Islands, about fifteen miles north-east from Rameo Islands. They have been extirpated by man; none having been seen for some years past. Halibuts abound more at the south-west coast than elsewhere. The young, in the fall, are one of the finest fishes on these coasts; but their excellence seems to be little known except to the fishermen and their families.

Part X. South Coast of Newfoundland—Termination of Journey.

December 14th. The coast was now everywhere clad in its white winter mantle, and most of the birds of passage had left the shores for a more genial climate. Having spent the night at the Rameo [Ramea] Islands, we set sail eastward, entering now upon the British Newfoundland coast. Passed by Little River, a good harbour, Cape La Hune, where two families reside, Bay Francois with three resident families; New Harbour, three resident families; Rencontre, four families, and Richard's Harbour, where several families reside in summer.

December 16th. Having been wind-bound one day in Richard's Harbour, a favouring breeze now carries us to the Bay of Despair, and in sight of the whaling and cod fishery establishment of Messrs. Newman, Hunt & Co. of London. The few inhabitants and their pursuits between Rameo and the Bay of Despair are similar to those farther to the westward. At the head of most of the harbours and bays, and along the margins of the waters that discharge into them, some good soil and spruce timber are to be found. Rock crystals of different colours are stated by the inhabitants to occur in quantities at Harbour le Cou and Diamond Cove in that neighbourhood. Several of the inhabitants possessed transparent specimens as curiosities.

Upon reaching the establishment of Messrs Newman & Co, at the Bay of Despair, I learnt with satisfaction that the last ship for England this season from this coast was to sail within a few days from another of their establishments in Fortune Bay. Harvey's boat and men now went back to the Dead Islands, but not without apprehension on my part for their safety, contending against westerly winds on this inhospitable coast at such a season. For while we were coming, with a fair wind, every drop of water and spray that came into our boat congealed as it fell, thus binding together boat, ropes, and sails in one mass of ice.

Here ended a four months' excursion of toil, pleasure, pain, and anxiety, succeeded by the delight of being again restored to society, which was enjoyed with the gentlemen and families of the mercantile establishments at the Bay of Despair and Fortune Bay.

It was impossible to reach St. John's, and I took passage at Little Bay, in Fortune, on the ship "Duck, sailing on the 28th of December, and arrived in Dartmouth, in England, on the 10th of February 1823."[115]

Other 19th-Century Travellers through Newfoundland's Interior

Though Cormack claimed that his trek was "the only one ever performed by a European,"[116] this statement has been disputed. Some suggest that the honour goes to Father William Herron (or Hearn).[117] Trained for the priesthood, Herron was sent to Placentia Bay, where he became responsible for the Catholics along the south and west coasts.[118] In 1820, after a visit to St. John's, where he performed five baptisms,[119] he went by sea to Notre Dame Bay. According to oral tradition, he walked from there to St. George's Bay "through trackless forests accompanied by a single Indian," but there appears to be no written record of the journey.

Later 19th-century travellers through Newfoundland's interior, whose exploits were recorded, include Mr. Rogers, a shipwreck victim of the *Fanny*, which struck the rocky shore in Port au Port Bay in November 1833. Together with two Mi'kmaq guides, he first walked to La Poile, but as the last ship had already left, he made his way to St. John's, probably on foot and by boat.[120] Archdeacon Edward Wix, whose visits to his charges, in 1835, took him to many far-flung places, would have been forced to walk large distances across the country.[121] In the winter of 1844, Mr. Salmon, an agent of Messrs. Slade & Co., walked on snowshoes, together with a companion, from Twillingate to Sandy Point and from there, with a Mi'kmaw guide, via Piper's Hole to St. John's. It took 31 days to cover about 375 kilometres as the crow flies.[122] N. O'Brig reported in his article "In Terre Neuve" that, in 1858, three English army officers crossed the island from Conception Bay to the Bay of Islands.[123] And in the winter of 1875, sawmill owner Joseph William Phillips of Point Leamington, who had urgent business in Toronto, made his way on snowshoes first to Bay d'Espoir and from there to St. John's. His story was retold by Don Morris in *The Express*, describing some of the tribulations Phillips met as "[w]olves, snow slides, met on 600-mile woods trek in 1875."[124]

Cormack Returns to Scotland

Cormack reached Glasgow early in 1823 and was confronted with the news that his stepfather, David Rennie, had died on January 7, 1823, at the age of 58.[125] According to the inventory of Rennie's personal estate, his properties in Scotland were valued at close to £14,000, plus land in Township 23 in Prince Edward Island. He bequeathed his estate to his five children: David Stuart, James Gower, William Frederick, Robert, and Janet Emma.[126] The Cormack siblings, David Rennie's stepchildren who had inherited the properties of their Cormack parents, were not mentioned in the will.

At the time of his stepfather's death, Cormack's brother, John Bell Cormack, was in a five-year apprenticeship in the law office of J.S. Robertson and J. Arnott in Edinburgh, having started in 1822. His "Law I" course at Edinburgh University had allowed him to become articled to a solicitor for further training. During his apprenticeship, in 1825, he also attended the "Law II" course and received the title of W.S. Writer of the Signet, in May 1827.[127] John Bell Cormack remained in Edinburgh practicing law until 1832.

In May 1824, Cormack's sister, Janet Grace Cormack, married William Scott, a merchant.[128] Before their wedding, the couple signed a marriage contract and disposition according to which William Scott renounced any claim to the estate of Janet Grace with regard to properties in Newfoundland, which had been assigned into a trust on behalf of the three Cormack children.[129] The couple moved to Naples and, of their nine children, the first three were born there. Around 1831 or 1832, the family moved to London.[130] Cormack kept in touch with his sister and, in 1850, when he was living in London, Janet's son, George, was asked to bring a New Zealand Moa bone to Professor Owen.[131]

Cormack's Account
of His Trek across Newfoundland in 1822

With the experience of his trek through Newfoundland's interior uppermost in his mind, Cormack spent the next few months in Glasgow writing a summary of his observations, entitled "Account of a Journey across the Island of Newfoundland." He also added to *Steel's Chart of Newfoundland's Southern Interior, 1817,* which he had used on his trek, the lakes and mountains with the place names he had bestowed, as well as geological formations. Professor Jameson in Edinburgh assisted him in identifying the rocks and minerals he had collected.[132] Cormack submitted the report and map through Jameson and John Barrow to the Right Honorable Earl Bathurst, Secretary of State for the Colonies.[133] His report was published in the *Edinburgh Philosophical Journal* in 1824.[134] The original manuscript has not survived, though Cormack's field map is preserved in the collection of the Centre for Newfoundland Studies at Memorial University.[135] His 1824 report covers little more than five printed pages. In it, Cormack briefly characterized the different parts of the island. Though he listed a few species of trees and shrubs with regard to "a botanical point of view," he believed the interior not "to be particularly interesting after having examined the country near the seacoast." Nevertheless, "the island altogether ... afforded a wide field for research to the botanist."[136] Cormack mentioned neither the personal experiences and deprivations that had hampered the two men's progress, nor did he refer to his return trip along the south coast to Fortune Bay. In later years, Cormack prepared longer accounts of the trek.

While his 1824 "Account of a Journey" had little immediate impact, perhaps at that time travels through the wilderness by one or two men with a guide were not particularly rare, but for many years to come Cormack's map remained a key source of information about the geography and geology of Newfoundland's central and southern interior. Geologists J.B. Jukes, Sir Richard Bonnycastle, and J.P. Howley used it in their reports, including Cormack's toponyms and geological notations.[137] In the 1970s, it was claimed that Cormack's "map of the interior was so precise that it was used in a survey for the trans-insular railway 50 years later."[138]

During his time in Britain, Cormack may also have written a paper entitled "On the Natural History and Economical Uses of the Cod, Capelin, Cuttle-Fish, and Seal, as they occur on the Banks of Newfoundland, and the Coasts of that Island and Labrador. Communicated in a Letter to Professor Jameson, by W.E. Cormack, Esq." (Appendix 1). It was published in the April–May 1826 the *Edinburgh New Philosophical Journal*. Cormack would have collected the information for this paper from fishers on the east as well as the west and south coasts of Newfoundland during his recovery in St. George's Bay and his trip along the south coast, using every opportunity to find out details about the fisheries in each area.

Residence in Newfoundland and Scotland, c.1823–1826

Cormack returned to St. John's in late 1823 or early 1824. At that time, he was involved in the shipping trade, as he owned the 120-ton brig *Brothers* that sailed between Liverpool and St. John's,[139] and was part-owner of the 42-ton schooner *Oak*.[140]

Cormack also started a commission business. In 1825 or earlier, he partnered with the Greenock merchant John B. Thompson in a company listed under the name Wm. E. Cormack & Co.[141] Together with Thompson, Cormack purchased the *Seven Sisters,* a 59-ton coastal Canadian schooner, which had been involved in the provisions and lumber trade from Canada. Thompson may have been particularly interested in the shipping trade rather than in Cormack's commission business, which sold goods on consignment for a commission. Between December 1825 and April 1826, the *Newfoundland Mercantile Journal* advertised split peas and pearl barley on sale by Cormack & Co.[142] In June 1826, the company advertised "250 Firkins excellent Irish Butter" sold for "Cash, fish or Oil."[143] Cormack also advertised for sale or rent "a Pew in the Established Church."[144]

As income, Cormack still received his share of the ground rents from his mother's trust disposition covering properties in St. John's. Additional income came from his properties in Prince Edward Island.

Despite his business obligations in Newfoundland, Cormack remained focused on his scientific interests. In the fall of 1825, he returned to Edinburgh University to take up further studies.[145] The University Class Lists for the period from fall 1825 to spring 1826 record him as attending a fifth-year literature class, as well as Professor Thomas Charles Hope's chemistry course.[146] It may be presumed that he had also contact with his former mentor, the renowned mineralogist Professor Jameson. One of his classmates in the chemistry course, and a student of Jameson, was Charles Darwin.[147]

Cormack returned in June 1826[148] to St. John's, where he, again, lived at the Roope's premises. While the commission sales continued, Cormack concentrated on research on the Newfoundland and Labrador fisheries. Although his paper "On the Natural History and Economical Uses of the Cod, Capelin, Cuttle-Fish, and Seal" focused on biological features,[149] he now presented a more political point of view. Mindful of the role that government should play in this area of commercial pursuit, Cormack accumulated data that showed the importance and value of Newfoundland's fisheries.[150]

Cormack Founds the Boeothick Institution in 1827

During his years in Newfoundland, Cormack would have heard reports about the persecution and dwindling numbers of the island's Indigenous people, the Beothuk. Originally a population of several hundreds who inhabited bays all around the island, they had by now lost much of their traditional habitat to incoming English and French settlers and the Mi'kmaq. Encounters had usually been hostile and the Beothuk, who defended themselves only with bow and arrows against enemies with firearms, were usually beaten. To avoid confrontations, they had gradually retired inland to areas around Red Indian Lake and the Exploits River, though they still visited the coast of Notre Dame Bay during spring and summer to hunt seal, harvest salmon, and procure seafoods. As they were still persecuted and killed, particularly by English settlers, their survival was no longer assured. Only three years before Cormack came to Newfoundland, the Beothuk woman Demasduit (called Mary March by the English) had been captured and taken to St. John's. John Peyton Jr., the magistrate who was living on Exploits Island, had led a party of men to a Beothuk camp at Red Indian Lake "to make peace with them" after the Beothuk had cut loose one of his boats. However, in the event the Beothuk chief, Nonosabasut, was killed trying to protect his wife, Demasduit, who had been captured.

When she was brought to St. John's, her gentleness and intelligence convinced citizens that the Beothuk were not the savages they were reported to be, an opinion that Cormack would have shared.

Sympathetic to their plight, Cormack wanted to save these "sylvian" people from extinction "for the sake of humanity."[151] In the fall of 1827, he decided to search for Beothuk survivors inland from Notre Dame Bay, known to be their last area of refuge, and to "force a friendly interview with some of them." According to a scribbled note in his papers, Cormack considered going with a large party—"self and others," including "4 Indians and 7 able men to be hired."[152] His stated objectives of the "Red Indian Expedition": to establish their numbers and means of subsistence. Cormack's undoubtedly ill-conceived plan was "to surround them and then advance upon them as friends or as their determined captors … persuade them by signs and drawings of our friendly intentions … that they must come with us to the coast."[153] This time, Cormack's equipment was to include "Mosquito veil, Mosquito ointment or mask of oil cloth with goggles, arrow points, small looking glasses, large beads and one seamless canoe-skin" to "carry two men."[154]

It so happened that A.W. Des Barres,[155] a senior assistant judge of the Supreme Court and judge of the Northern Circuit Court was travelling to Twillingate to attend to his judicial duties.[156] Having heard about Cormack's intent to travel to Exploits Island, he offered Cormack a berth on his vessel. Once in Twillingate, on October 2, 1827, Cormack organized a meeting at the courthouse of men interested in the cause of the Beothuk. He described to the assembled group how the Beothuk had been widely persecuted and appealed to feelings of guilt and sympathy by asserting that "those who are invested with power and influence in society" are all the more obligated "to reclaim the aborigines from their present hapless condition" and "bring about justice."[157] A society to be called the "Boeothick Institution" for the "purpose of opening a communication with, and promoting the civilization of the Red Indians of Newfoundland" was proposed, an idea that had originated with Des Barres.[158]

The institution was to be supported by voluntary subscriptions and donations. The bishop of Nova Scotia, John Inglis,[159] was voted patron and the Honourable Augustus Wallet Des Barres vice-patron. Cormack became president and treasurer, John Dunscombe[160] vice-president, and John Stark[161] secretary. The positions of honorary vice-patrons were assigned to Professor Jameson, Cormack's mentor in Edinburgh, and to John Barrow, Esq., one of the secretaries to the Admiralty in Britain. John Peyton Jr., justice of the peace and merchant at Exploits Island, was voted resident agent and corresponding member.[162] It was proposed that the Beothuk woman "Shanawdithit," at that time living with the Peytons, "be placed under the paternal care of the institution, the expense of her support and education to be provided for out of general funds." Peyton Jr. had taken Shanawdithit into his household

in 1823 after she and her mother and sister were taken prisoner by several settlers, and the mother and sister had meanwhile died. At that time, aged 30, Peyton Jr. had just married his 17-year-old bride, Eleanor, who must have found it difficult to handle the captive.

FIGURE 3. PORTRAIT OF SHANAWDITHIT.

In a letter to Stark, Cormack reflected on the success of the meeting, reminding him of "the ever memorable and glorious day at Twillingate, when the oldest and most respectable inhabitants of the place reluctantly left the dinner table of the Court to breakfast with their families,"[163] suggesting that the discussion had continued throughout the night.

Cormack later rejected the bishop of Nova Scotia's suggestion to name Governor Sir Thomas Cochrane as patron of the Boeothick Institution,[164] presumably because Cochrane had neither acknowledged Cormack's successful 1822 trek across the island, nor the aims of the Institution, and had shown no interest in the care of Shanawdithit. Indeed, Cormack accused the government of gross negligence of the island's Indigenous inhabitants, stating, in well-intentioned though colonialist language of the time, "[i]t is a melancholy reflection that our local Government has been such that under it the extirpation of a whole Tribe of primitive fellow creatures has taken place."[165]

Cormack's Trek Inland in Search of Beothuk in November 1827

By the time his search for Beothuk survivors became a reality, Cormack had abandoned the idea of taking hired men, most likely due to lack of government support and financial considerations. Having been unable to get in touch with Joseph Sylvester through his contact, Wm. Creed in Galtois,[166] he engaged John Louis, an Abenaki;[167] Maurice Louis, a young Mi'kmaq;[168] and an elderly Montagnais, John Stevens.[169] It had been difficult to obtain men fit for the purpose, and the trouble attending to this task had prevented Cormack from starting the expedition a month earlier in the season. The bishop of Nova Scotia believed that it would not be safe to rely entirely on Indigenous men as his crew,[170] but Cormack was satisfied to go with his guides and defended their reputation in a lengthy note that forms part of his papers.[171] It has been suggested that Cormack's trust in his guides set a lasting example and initiated the custom among hunters and others to turn to Indigenous men when looking for guides through Newfoundland's wilderness.

As Cormack had plans to leave for Britain to lay the proceedings of the Boeothick Institution before the Earl of Bathurst, Secretary of State for the Colonial Department,[172] he initially prepared only a brief outline of the expedition, which was read at a meeting of the Institution by its chairman, A.W. Des Barres. He later wrote a more extensive report, which he read before the Institution in January 1828. It was subsequently published in the *Edinburgh New Philosophical Journal* in 1829.[173] It is this longer report which J.P. Howley published in *The Beothucks or Red Indians,* which is presented here in an abbreviated form:[174]

My party consisted of three Indians, viz. an intelligent and able man of the Abenakie tribe from Canada; an elderly Mountaineer from Labrador; and an adventurous young Mikmak, a native of this island, together with myself. Our equipment was similar to that used on my previous trip which I had found eminently suitable. However, this time we reduced provisions because we expected to subsist largely on caribou and beaver which we planned to shoot on the way. We stayed for a few days as guests of the Peytons on Exploits Island. Our host was absent but had placed a boat and crew at our disposal. It was my intention to have commenced our search at White Bay and to have travelled southward from there, but the weather did not permit us to reach White Bay. This caused several days delay, and eventually I unwillingly changed our route.

On the 31st of October 1827, we entered the country at the mouth of the River Exploits, at the Northern Arm. We took a north-westerly direction to lead us to Hall's Bay, which place we reached through an almost uninterrupted forest in hilly country, in eight days.

However, on the fourth day after our departure, at a portage at the east end of Badger Bay Great Lake, known as the Indian path, we found traces of the Red Indians. There was a canoe-rest with daubs of red-ochre, also a spear shaft, eight feet in length doubted with red ochre, parts of old canoes, fragments of skin-dresses & for some distance around, the trunks of the birch and spruce trees had been rinded, these people using the inner part of the bark for food. Some of the cuts of the trees done with an axe were evidently made the previous year. The traces left by the Red Indians are so peculiar that we were confident those we saw were made by them.

This spot is situated at the commencement of a portage, which leads from the seacoast at Badger Bay about eight miles to the north-east, and to a chain of lakes extending westerly and southerly from here eventually discharging themselves by a rivulet into the River Exploits. Another path leads from here to the lakes near New Bay to the eastward. Here were the remains of one of their villages, where the vestiges of eight or ten winter mamateeks (or wigwams), each intended to contain from six to eighteen or twenty people, were seen close together. There were also remains of summer wigwams. Every winter wigwam had close by a small square-mouthed pit, about four feet deep, to preserve their stores in. We also discovered the remains of a vapour-bath. The Boeothick's method to use such a bath was to light a fire for heating stones, and when they were hot to remove the ashes and place a hemispherical framework of skins closely over it. The patient then crept in under the skins and, by pouring water on the hot stones, raised the steam.

At Hall's Bay we got no useful information from the three English families settled there. Indeed, we could hardly have expected any for it was people like these who have been the unchecked destroyers of the tribe. After a night at a house, we struck into the country again and in five days were on the highlands south of White Bay. It was now near the middle of November and the winter had commenced severely in the interior. The country was everywhere covered with snow, and for some days past, we had walked over the small ponds on the ice. The deer were migrating from the rugged and dreary mountains in the north to the low mossy barrens and more woody parts in the south and we inferred that if any of the Red Indians had been at White Bay during the past summer, they might be at this time stationed at the deer passes killing deer for winter provisions. Such passes in the migration lines would be at the extreme end of lakes, the foot of valleys between high or rugged mountains, fords in the large rivers and the like. Here, the Boeothick kill great numbers of deer with very little trouble.

We looked out for two days from the summits of the adjacent hills trying to discover the smoke from their camps, but in vain. We now determined to proceed towards the Red Indian's Lake, sanguine that we would find the objects of our search. In about ten days we got a glimpse of this beautiful majestic and splendid sheet of water. We looked down on the lake with feelings of anxiety and admiration. But no canoe could be discovered moving on its placid surface. We approached the lake with hope and caution; but found to our mortification that the Red Indians had deserted it for some years past. My party had been so exited and determined to obtain an interview of some kind with these people, that on discovering from appearances everywhere around us, that the

Red Indians no longer existed, the spirits of one and all of us were deeply affected. The old Mountaineer was particularly overcome. This had long been the central and undisturbed rendezvous of the tribe when they had enjoyed peace and security. But they now had abandoned it, after being tormented by parties of Europeans during the last 18 years. Unfortunately, fatal rencounters had on these occasions taken place.

We spent several melancholy days wandering on the borders of the lake, surveying the various remains of what we now contemplated to have been an unoffending and cruelly extirpated race. At several places, small clusters of winter and summer wigwams were found in ruins. One peculiarity of the wigwams was the fact that they had small hollows, like nests, dug in the earth around the fireplace, one for each person to sit in. These hollows are generally so close together and to the fireplace and the sides of the wigwam that I think it probable these people have been accustomed to sleep in a sitting position.

There was one wooden building for drying and smoking venison, in still perfect condition; a small log house used for storage, but now dilapidated; and the wreck of a twenty-two feet birch rind canoe, thrown up among the bushes at the beach. All the birch trees in the vicinity of the lake and many spruce fir had the bark taken off to use for food.

We also came upon a cemetery. Their wooden repositories for the dead were in the most perfect state of preservation. In one of them, resembling a hut ten feet by eight and in every way well secured against the weather and the intrusion of wild beasts, two grown persons were laid out at full length on the floor; the bodies were wrapped round with deer skins. One of them appeared to have been placed here not longer ago than five or six years. We thought there were children laid in here also. On first opening this building our curiosity was raised to the highest pitch, but what added to our surprise was the discovery of a white deal coffin, containing a skeleton neatly shrouded in muslin. After much conjecture, the idea of Mary March occurred to one of the party and the whole mystery was at once explained. In this hut were also deposited a variety of articles. There were two small wooden images of a man and woman, a small doll, several small models of their canoes, two small models of boats, an iron axe, a bow and quiver of arrows, as also two fire-stones, various kinds of culinary utensils neatly made of birch rind and ornamented, and many other things some of which we did not know the use or meaning.

Another mode of sepulchre was where the body of the deceased had been wrapped in birch rind, and with his property, placed on a sort of scaffold formed of four posts, about seven feet high, and fixed perpendicularly in the ground to sustain a kind of crib on which the body and property rested.

A third mode was, where the body was bent together and wrapped in birch rind, was laid on its right side, and enclosed in a kind of box, about four feet by three, and two and a half deep, and placed on the ground.

A fourth, and the most common mode of burying, has been to have the body wrapped in birch rind, placed on the ground or a couple of feet under the surface of the earth and then covered with a heap of stones.

These people appear to have always shewn great respect for their dead. The most remarkable burying places commonly observed by Europeans are at the seacoast. They are particularly chosen spots, and it is well known that these people have been in the habit of bringing their dead from a distance to these locations.

On the north side of the lake, opposite the River Exploits, are the extremities of two deer fences, about half a mile apart, where they lead to the water. These fences diverge many miles into the country in a north-westerly direction. The Red Indians make these fences to lead and scare the deer to the lake during their periodical migration. When the deer get into the water to swim across, the Beothuk attack and kill the animals with spears out of their canoes. In this way they secure their winter provisions before the severity of that season sets in.

One night we encamped on the foundation of an old Red Indian wigwam. A large fire at night is the life and soul of such a party as ours, and when it blazed up at times, I could not help observing that two of my guides evinced uneasiness and want of confidence in things around, as if they thought themselves usurpers of the Red Indian territory. This lake and the areas adjacent have always been considered to belong exclusively to the Red Indians and to have been occupied only by them.

Our only and frail hope now left of seeing the Red Indians lay on the banks of the River Exploits. The Red Indian's Lake discharges itself about three or four miles from its north-east end and its waters form the River Exploits. From the lake to the seacoast is considered about seventy miles; and down this noble river the steady perseverance and intrepidity of my guides carried me on rafts in four days, to accomplish what would otherwise have probably required two weeks. We landed at various places on both banks of the river on our way down but found no traces of the Red Indians as recent as those seen at the portage at Badger Bay Great Lake towards the beginning of our journey. During our descent, we had to construct new rafts at the different waterfalls. Sometimes we were carried down the rapids at the rate of ten miles an hour or more, with considerable risks of destruction to the whole party, for we were always together on one raft.

What arrests the attention most, while gliding down the stream, is the extent of the fences to entrap the deer. They extend from the lake downwards, continuous on the banks of the river at least thirty miles. There are openings left here and there in them for the animals to go through and swim across the river and at these places the Beothuk are stationed and kill them in the water out of their canoes. Here then, connecting these fences with those on the north-side of the lake, is at least forty miles of country easterly and westerly, prepared to intercept all the deer that pass that way in their periodical migrations. It was melancholy to contemplate the gigantic, yet feeble efforts of a whole primitive nation, in their anxiety to provide subsistence, forsaken and going to decay.

There must have been hundreds of the Red Indians, and that not many years ago, to have kept up these fences and pounds. As their numbers were lessened so was their ability to keep them up for the purposes intended; and now the deer pass the whole line unmolested. We infer, that the few of those people who yet survive have taken refuge in some sequestered spot in the northern part of the island where they can procure deer to subsist on.

On 29th of November we again returned to the mouth of the River Exploits, in thirty days after our departure from there having made a complete circuit of about 200 miles in the Red Indian territory.

Cormack returned to the house of John Peyton, magistrate of Twillingate, who knew him intimately. Peyton later told Howley that he saw Cormack just as he was about to enter the interior on his journey in 1827 and again on his return. At first, he could scarcely recognize in the tall, gaunt, shaggy individual who stood before him the man whom he had seen a few months previous to his start, full of life and vigour, clean, kempt, and well kept. His appearance now betokened what the man had gone through in the interim.

Cormack Presents His Report at a Meeting of the Boeothick Institution

At a meeting of the Boeothick Institution, Cormack presented his report of the search for Beothuk survivors and congratulated the Institution for possessing not only a number of Beothuk artifacts, such as models of their canoes, bows and arrows, spears, and other items, but also a vocabulary of 200 to 300 words of the Beothuk language—presumably a copy of the Demasduit wordlist he would have received from Peyton Jr. He also mentioned that materials collected on this and his previous excursion across the interior—probably rocks and plants—provided new knowledge about the natural condition and production of the interior of Newfoundland. However, he later gave the Beothuk artifacts, with the exception of the vocabulary, to Jameson for the University Museum in Edinburgh.[175]

Cormack suggested that it would be best from now on to employ Indians belonging to the other tribes to search for remnants of the Beothuk in areas that had not yet been covered. He had already chosen three of the most intelligent men from among those he met with in Newfoundland to follow up this search.

It was therefore resolved that the measures recommended in the president's report be agreed to and that the three men, Indians of the Canadian and Mountaineer tribes, be placed upon the establishment of this Institution to be employed under the immediate direction of the president, and that they be allowed for their services such a sum of money as the president may consider a fair and reasonable compensation.

He also suggested that "this Institution should endeavour to collect every useful information respecting the natural production and resources of this island, and from time to time publish the same in its reports."

That the instruction of Shanawdithit, the Beothuk woman who had been captured by a couple of settlers and now lives with John Peyton Jr. and his family on Exploits Island would be much accelerated by bringing her to St. John's.

When the Indian female Shawnawdithit arrives in St. John's I would recommend that a correct likeness be taken, and be preserved in the records of the institution.

That the proceedings of the Institution since its establishment be laid before his Majesty's Secretary of State for the Colonial Department, the Earl of Bathurst, by the President, on his arrival in England."[176]

Cormack asked John Stark, secretary of the Boeothick Institution, to have the report of the meeting in Twillingate published in *The Royal Gazette* so that the town's citizens were informed of his efforts to approach the Beothuk. Stark privately sent a copy to Mr. Barrow, a copy to a Liverpool newspaper, and one to Sir Charles Hamilton.[177] Cormack also thought the cost of carrying out the objectives of the Institution would run to £250 annually, and that the officers of the Institution would have to exert themselves to raise sufficient funds.[178] To do his share, Stark was going to approach members of the Institution in Harbour Grace but wanted to wait for the completion of a successful seal fishery, which would encourage patrons to donate more money.[179]

The Search for Beothuk Carried Out by Three Indian Men, Starting in Spring 1828

In agreement with the decision of the Boeothick Institution to send from now on Indian men to look for Beothuk survivors, Cormack instructed the men he had already chosen as follows:

John Louis, the leader of the party, is to proceed to Clode Sound in Bonavista Bay to inform John Stevens and Peter John that they have been nominated as the most proper persons for this job. John Louis will then arrange that they start from Fortune Bay on or before the tenth day of March next (in 1828). They are first to proceed to White Bear Bay to consult with the Mi'kmaq there and from thence proceed through the country to St. George's Bay, then to the Bay of Islands Lake (Grand Lake), then pass to the west of Red Indian Lake and from there northward to White Bay, and then return to the River Exploits and wait on John Peyton Jr. and the Rev. Mr. Chapman for further instructions.

Any communication with the Boeothick ought to be avoided to exclude the possibility of an unfriendly interchange. John Louis and his party will therefore at all times avoid coming in contact with the Red Indians however favourable the meeting may appear to be. They will, however, endeavour to ascertain as correctly as they possibly can the numbers of the Red Indians now in existence and the country occupied by them, and will then immediately return to St. John's to report the particulars of their discovery in order that another expedition upon a more matured plan, and other measures may be adopted by the Institution.[180]

In May 1828, Cormack received a report from Fortune Bay that John Louis had been joined by the two other men. They had left on March 27 in pursuit of the Red Indians and seemed to be almost confident of finding them.[181] But a month later, Cormack was informed that the three men had returned without being able to establish whether any of the Beothuk had survived.[182]

Meeting of Members of the Boeothick Institution on June 24, 1828

At a meeting of the subscribers to the Boeothick Institution on June 24, 1828, Cormack was called upon to give an account of the endeavours of the search party:

John Louis had left St. John's on February 12 and had proceeded to Clode Sound where John Stevens and Peter John joined him. They travelled to Bay Despair to collect information from the Mi'kmaq and proceeded from there to St. George's Bay and to the Great Bay of Islands Lake (Grand Lake) without discovering any recent signs of the Red Indians. After leaving this lake, the party moved on to Red Indian Lake where they constructed another canoe and spent upwards of a week examining the different creeks and coves but with the same ill success. They then paddled down the Exploits River and two days later reached Mr. Peyton Jr.'s upper establishment where they procured a passage back to St. John's. It took the men four months to complete the trip. They arrived here 4 days ago.[183]

It appeared that the party had examined the whole of the country in the interior where the Red Indians were likely to be found except for the vicinity of White Bay, a large tract of land which remained unexplored. Cormack suggested the following measures, which were unanimously approved of by the members of the Institution:

That the three Indians be again employed to explore and examine the country in the interior of and adjacent to White Bay; and that I be authorised to employ one of the European settlers to accompany them. (In the event this did not materialize.)

As they will now explore a part of the island contiguous to the French fisheries, it would prove beneficial to enquire with the French people and solicit the aid of the French Commandant in the progress of their search.

To give the party an increased incentive to search thoroughly the men should be promised a gratuity of $150 in addition to their monthly pay upon their discovery of the abode of Red Indians now living.

The friends of the Institution should also be requested again to contribute in support of this new exploration. Considering that the plans for the new search will involve considerably more work, William Thomas should be asked to accept the office of Treasurer to the Institution.

The Search for Beothuk Carried out by Three Native Men, Starting in Spring 1828

Later in the year John Louis, John Stevens, and Peter John were sent out again. According to my instructions the party was to board the schooner Eclipse and disembark at Croque Harbour. John Louis was to deliver a letter to the French Commandant, requesting him to give any information that may lead to the discovery of some of the Red Indians. If any of them were said to be in the vicinity, John Louis was required to apply for written directions as to where he would most likely find some of them. The party should then proceed to examine that area. If they were unable to discover any of the Indians to the north of Croque Harbour, they were to move west into the interior for about twenty miles, and then take a southwardly direction to White Bay, pass around the head of White Bay, and then in the most proper direction search through the country on the way to the house of Mr. Peyton, the resident agent at Exploits Burnt Island, being careful to examine the whole of the lakes, rivers, and country along the route described. The party must be able to give the most unequivocal information that no part of the country has been left unsearched. I also request John Louis to make a plan of the country (a bark map) he has passed over, marking down every lake, river, and mountain, so that Mr. Peyton who is intimately acquainted with the interior may be able to afford the Institution his opinion and observation thereon.

Cormack also wrote a letter to the French commandant, explaining

the condition of the Red Indians and the attempt of the newly formed Boeothick Institution to find the remnant of these people and open a friendly intercourse with them. A party from among the other tribes, after having unsuccessfully searched for them from St. George's Bay to Red Indian Lake and the Exploits River, had now been charged to look for their abodes in the area of White Bay and to the north of it to determine their existence or extinction. The Society [the Boeothick Institution] would request his good offices in affording any facilities to this mission and would be thankful for any information he may be able to give the search party relating to the Red Indians.

The three men had proceeded to the French Shore and examined the northern parts of the island. At Croque, the French commandant afforded them every assistance that might further their object, in men, boats, ammunition, and provisions, and the same facilities were secured by them along the whole French shoreline. The French authorities could give them no information of any trace of the Red Indians having been seen in the neighbourhood of their fisheries. From the head of White Bay, the search party had taken a southeastern direction and again came out at the seacoast in Notre Dame Bay, discovering nothing on their whole route indicative of any of the Red Indians having been recently alive in these parts. But old marks abounded everywhere from White Bay to Notre Dame Bay. The three men concluded that, if any Beothuk still existed, their number would be very small and it would not be prudent to send armed men again to search for them.[184]

Having been confident that the Red Indians could be contacted and saved from extinction and having spent a considerable amount of energy and resources to prove this point, Cormack was deeply disappointed to find that all efforts had been in vain. However, as Bishop Inglis and Stark were to say, "he had reason to feel some satisfaction in having done his utmost in the general cause of humanity."[185]

Shanawdithit Placed under the Care of the Boeothick Institution in 1828

When John Louis and his men returned from their second unsuccessful search for Beothuk survivors, Cormack realized that Shanawdithit, who was still living with the Peytons, was the only person who could provide authentic information about her people's history, language, and customs. He considered it therefore a priority to transfer Shanawdithit to St. John's.

In accordance with the resolution of the Boeothick Institution to place Shanawdithit under the care of the Institution, Stark and Andrew Pearce went in Pearce's yacht to the Peytons on Exploits Island to pick up Shanawdithit. But Mrs. Peyton said that "Shanawdithit's things were not quite ready," and they left without her.[186] A few days later, Mrs. Peyton, "who seems to have been quite willing for Shanawdithit to come away," sent a boat with her to Twillingate. Mrs. Peyton may have had reasons for not objecting to letting her go. In 1823, John Peyton Jr. had taken Shanawdithit into his household a few months after he had married 17-year-old Eleanor.[187] It must have been difficult for the young Mrs. Peyton to deal with an Indigenous captive who was six or more years her senior, who could be pert and openly defy her, and at times go into sulky moods and disappear into the woods for days.[188] Shanawdithit had also developed a cough that was not getting better, and Mrs. Peyton may have thought that she could get help for her illness in St. John's.

In Twillingate, Shanawdithit stayed with the Reverend and Mrs. Chapman, who were very kind to her. When the opportunity arose, Mr. Abbott offered Shanawdithit a passage on his boat to St. John's, and on September 20, 1828, he delivered her with Cormack at the Roope premises.[189]

John Peyton Jr. was much displeased about Shanawdithit's removal from his household in his absence—perhaps he was afraid that she would talk about his father's murder of Beothuk 14 or 15 years previously.[190] But Cormack defended the transfer, saying that "when you were here in summer, there was a good deal said about bringing her round to instruct her, and it was intended to mention it to you as a proposition, but it was delayed day after day until you had gone."[191] Cormack was determined to salvage what Shanawdithit was able to communicate and seems to have expected Peyton Jr. to share his view, stating that "it was done for the best and with the best intentions."[192]

Stark, who was greatly worried about Shanawdithit's well-being, had several suggestions about her safety. He thought she should be placed under the care of a steady woman and that a stout watch be kept over her morals. No one should be allowed to see her without special permission. She should immediately be vaccinated. She should also be given new clothes, as they were much cheaper in St. John's.[193] Stark apologized for giving advice since he knew Cormack to be a man of sound sense and discriminating knowledge of human nature, yet he felt impelled to make sure that everything would be done for Shanawdithit's safety. He also thought that the great interest taken in her by Attorney General James Simms would render him particularly well fitted, being a married man, to advise what to do. To please Nancy (the name the settlers had given her), Stark gave her a separate note for Cormack with the following text:

Dear Cormack, this note will I trust be handed to you by the Red Indian Shanawdithit herself. She asked me if you had any family, and I told her that when I left St. John's you were single but that I could not tell how long you would remain so. Above all things I request you will get her vaccinated by Doctor Carson upon the very day she reaches St. John's, pray let nothing prevent this. Yours faithfully John Stark.[194]

Assuming responsibility for Shanawdithit's well-being included having Dr. William Carson look after her health.[195] She was said to be suffering from consumption and during the nine months under the care of the Boeothick Institution to have often been unwell.[196] Cormack is believed to have commissioned the well-known artist William Gosse to paint a portrait of her, something he had already advocated in his report to the Institution about his search for the Red Indians.[197] This portrait is now exhibited in The Rooms—her penetrating and reproachful look is striking.[198]

When Bishop Inglis, who had met Shanawdithit, visited the Peytons in 1827, he described her as a "graceful woman, about 23 years old, with a mild and pleasing countenance and a fine disposition."[199] He also noted that "Peyton's children loved her and would leave their mother to run to her."[200] Cormack later described her as "having a lively disposition and a strong sense of gratitude and showed great affection for her parents and friends."[201]

The following description was written by Cormack's friend John MacGregor in his article "Sketches of Savage Life," published anonymously in 1836.[202] Cormack must have stayed with MacGregor previously as well as after his trek across the island of Newfoundland

and would have left records about the story of the Beothuk and the drawings by Shanawdithit with him when he moved to Glasgow in 1823. MacGregor had never seen Shanawdithit and would have relied on Cormack's words and Shanawdithit's drawings, possibly including a self-portrait. These are his words:

> Her name in her own language was pronounced Shaa-naan-dithit. She was the last of the Boeothics. Her person, in height above the middle stature, possessed classical regularity of form. Her face bore striking similarity to that of Napoleon, and the olive cast of her complexion added to the resemblance. Her hair was jet black; her finely pencilled brows—her long, darting lashes her dark, vigilant and piercing eyes were all remarkably striking and beautiful. Her teeth were white, even, and perfectly sound. Her hands and feet, small and well formed. She never laughed. Her smile was an exertion to do so, not a feeling.
>
> Her manners were easy and graceful, her temper generally calm; but on occasion, when some of the servants treated her, as she thought, with disrespect, her fierce Indian spirit kindled— the savage eye darted fire and vengeance; and the uniform kindness of Mr. Cormack alone would subdue the tempest which raged in the bosom of Shanawdithit.[203]

Dr. Carson characterized Shanawdithit as "a tall, strong, female … of amicable disposition, tractable, high spirited and proud. She felt most keenly the slightest degradation. My acquaintance with her and the still more interesting female Mary March gave me a high opinion of the disposition and abilities of the Red Indians."[204]

When Shanawdithit arrived with Cormack, she spoke little English, and it became a priority to instruct her in the English language. He provided her with paper and pencils and found that she had a talent for drawing.[205] When questioned about encounters of her people with Europeans, Shanawdithit produced sketches of events, such as the arrival of Buchan's party at a Beothuk camp on Red Indian Lake in the winter of 1810–11 (Sketch I, Figure 4), including the victory feast after two of Buchan's men had been decapitated.[206] Sketch II (Figure 5) depicts the taking of Demasduit (known as Mary March by the settlers) by the party of John Peyton Jr. and Sr. and several of their men.[207] Shanawdithit disclosed later that in the encounter they not only killed Demasduit's husband, Chief Nonosabasut, but also his brother. She sketched Buchan's party going up the Exploits River with Demasduit's

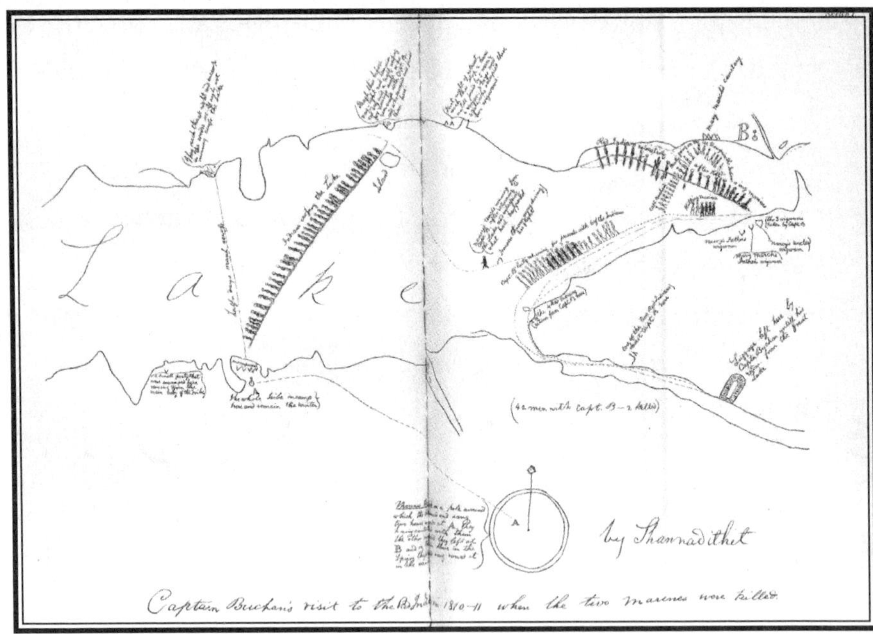

FIGURE 4. SHANAWDITHIT'S SKETCH I: CAPTAIN BUCHAN'S VISIT TO BEOTHUK CAMP AT RED INDIAN LAKE, WHERE HIS TWO MARINES WERE KILLED.

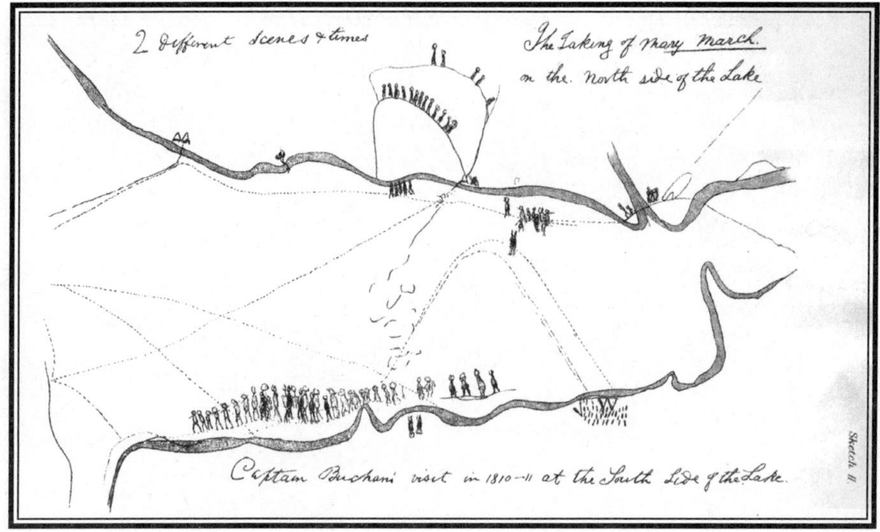

FIGURE 5. SHANAWDITHIT'S SKETCH II: CAPTURE OF DEMASDUIT ON RED INDIAN LAKE.

remains in Sketch III[208] and the location where a Beothuk woman was killed by Peyton Sr. 14 or 15 years prior to that, in Sketch V.[209] Most revealing is Sketch IV (Figure 6), marking the camps of Beothuk families and their route as they moved from the Exploits River to the lakes inland from Badger Bay in March–April 1823.[210] Cormack's notes include further details of the Beothuk's situation, their experiences with the English, a census of the different Beothuk groups in 1811, their decline and amalgamation, and the number of Beothuk who died prior to Shanawdithit's capture, in 1823.[211] At that time, only 12 of her kin were left; she never narrated this part of her story without tears.

Shanawdithit also drew Beothuk winter and summer mamateeks and other structures (Sketch VI, Figure 7),[212] a variety of animal food items (Sketch VII),[213] and various objects, including a woman in what appears to be a dancing dress (Sketch VIII).[214] She drew a picture of Cormack's dwelling house at Roope's Plantation (Sketch X, Figure

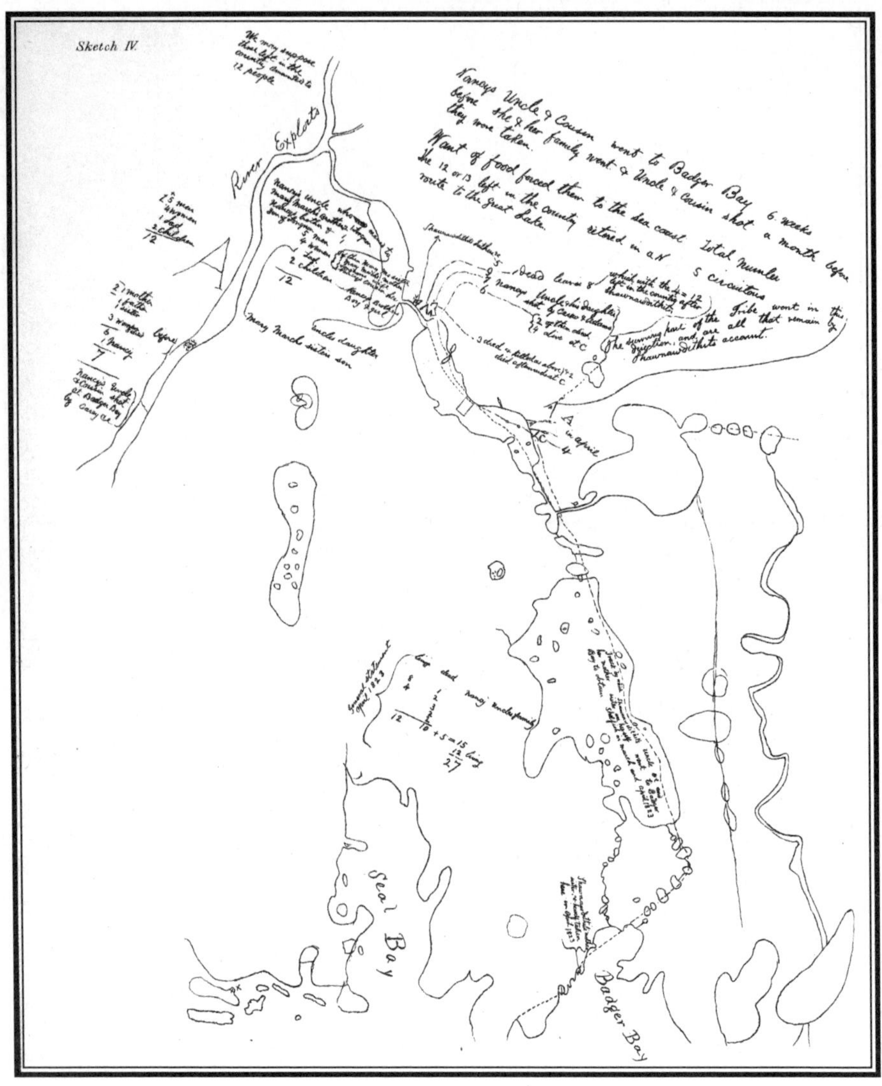

FIGURE 6. SHANAWDITHIT'S SKETCH IV: BEOTHUK CAMPS ON BADGER
BAY RIVER.

9),[215] showing the front and back of the house next to each other.
Sketch IX (Figure 8) is a drawing of Emblems of Mythology. In a letter
to Bishop John Inglis, Cormack wrote: "I have lately discovered the
key to the Mythology of her tribe," but there is no further information

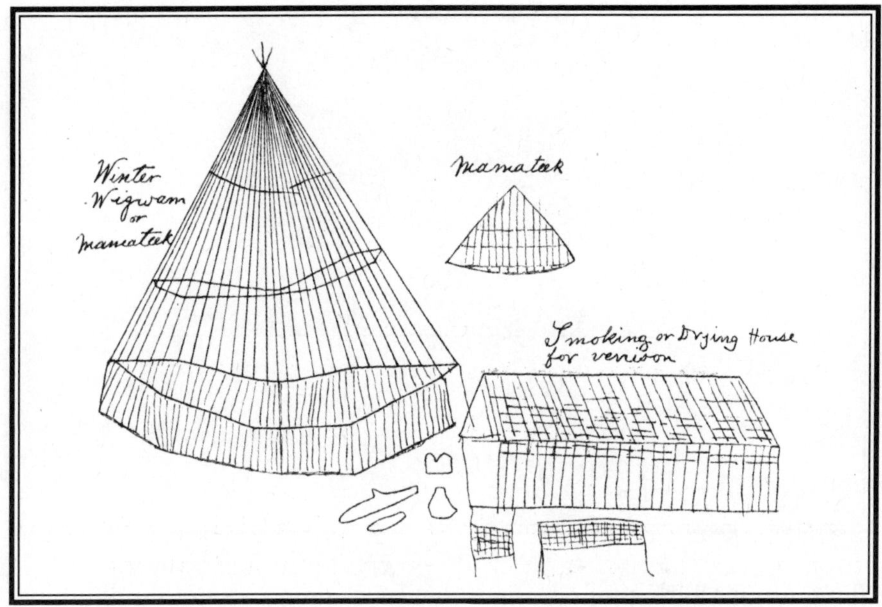

FIGURE 7. SHAWNAWDITHIT'S SKETCH VI, SUMMER AND WINTER MAMTEEKS, SMOKING HOUSE.

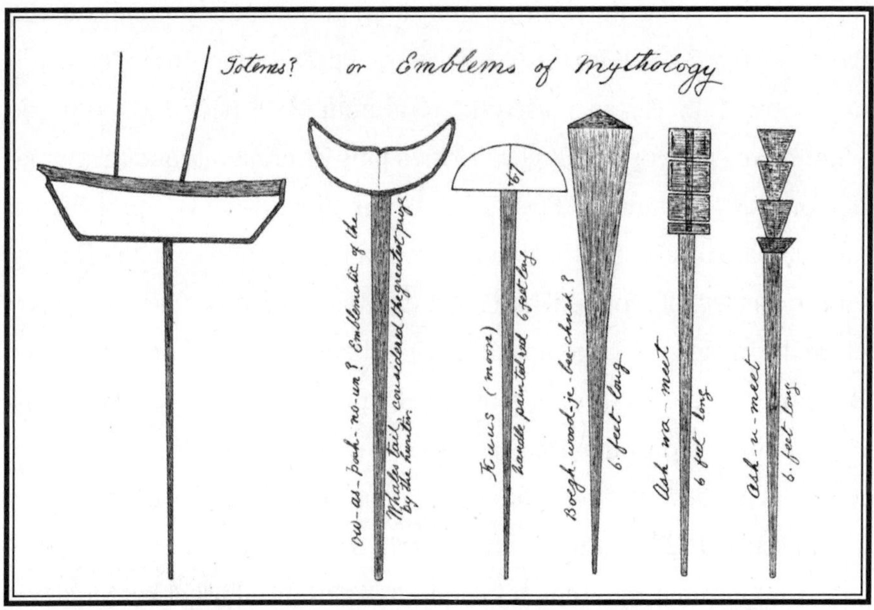

FIGURE 8. SHAWNAWDITHIT'S SKETCH IX: MYTHOLOGICAL EMBLEMS.

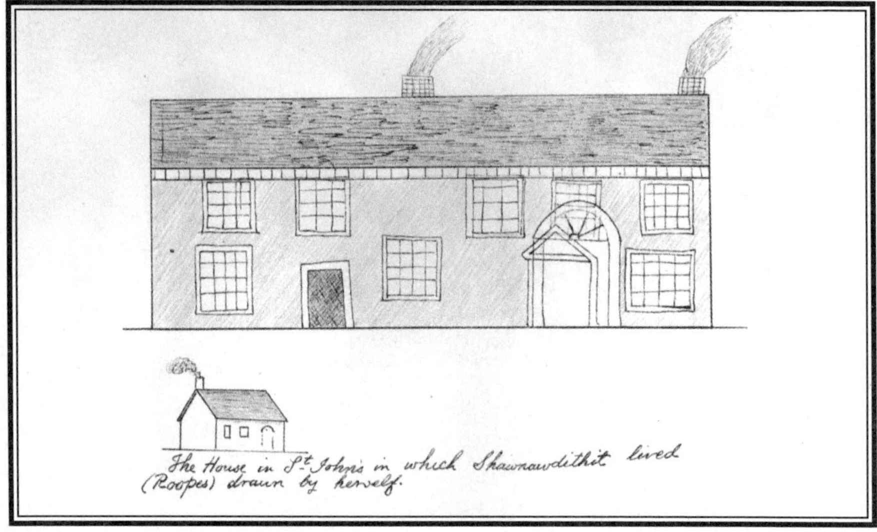

FIGURE 9. SHAWNADITHIT'S SKETCH X: DWELLING HOUSE AT ROOPE'S PLANTATION.

about his discovery of the meaning of the symbols among his papers.[216]

Cormack collected from Shanawdithit a vocabulary of about 120 words not included in the wordlists acquired earlier from Oubee[217] and Demasduit. This increased the total number of Beothuk words and phrases we know to 325 English glosses plus 21 numerals and the names of months.[218] In January 1829, Cormack submitted what was probably an amalgamated list of Beothuk words from all three sources to the Natural History Society of Montreal as a token of his appreciation for having been elected corresponding member,[219] saying that these words came from the Beothuk woman who was at that time living in his house. He also gave a copy of this wordlist to a Dr. Yates, probably Dr. James Yates,[220] whom he might have known from his university days in Glasgow in 1811.

In early 1829, Cormack transferred Shanawdithit to the home of Attorney General Simms and his family. As a parting gift, she presented him with a rounded piece of granite, a piece of quartz, and a lock of her hair.[221]

Nothing is known about Shanawdithit's life while she stayed with the Simms family, other than that Dr. Carson continued to look after her health. But when his medical ministrations could no longer halt the steady progress of her consumption, she was moved to the St. John's hospital located in the area of today's Victoria Park.[222] Shanawdithit died there on June 6, 1829. According to J.K. Kent, in a letter to John Peyton Jr., "she died of consumption, and the medical men of this town for the benefit of science dissected her body." After her skull was examined, it was sent to the Royal College of Physicians in London for further study.[223] It was later transferred to the Royal College of Surgeons and was subsequently destroyed in an air raid during World War II.[224]

Cormack's obituary for the *London Times*, published September 14, 1829, was largely a requiem on the disappearance of the Beothuk. He wrote: "There has been a primitive nation, once claiming rank as a portion of the human race, who have lived, flourished, and become extinct in their own orbit. They have been dislodged, and disappeared from the earth in their native independence in 1829."[225]

Shanawdithit was buried in the old cemetery on the south side of St. John's harbour. Presumably this was the burial ground attached to the military hospital located several hundred metres west of where the parish church of St. Mary the Virgin was built in 1859.[226] A plaque attached to a cairn close to this church contains these words: "Near this spot is the burying place of Nancy Shanawdithit very probably the last of the aborigines who died on June 6th 1829."[227]

Among the Cormack Papers is the note: "I have been favoured by Mr. W.H. Rennie with the following poem written by the celebrated New England poet, I.C. Whittier [should be J.G.], Haverhill, Mass. Nov.

1829, and inscribed to W.E. Cormack Esq. It refers to Shanawdithit 'the last of the Beothucks, or Red Indians.' Mr. Rennie received it from his cousin Mr. Charles Scott of Alverstoke, Hant":[228]

An Indian girl and the last of the Red Indians, or Beoethics, recently died in St. John's, Newfoundland. Her tribe, the Aborigines of Newfoundland, never held intercourse with any other tribe, or with the Europeans around them.[229]

"The Indian Girl's Lament,"
by John Greenleaf Whittier.[230]

The moons of autumn wax and wane; the hollow sound of floods
Is borne upon the mournful wind and broadly on the woods;
The changes of the changeful leaves—those painted flowers of frost
Before the round and yellow sun, how beautiful are tossed.

The morning breaketh with the same broad pencilling of sky
And blushes through its golden clouds as the great sun goes by;
And evening lingers in the west, more beautiful than dreams
That whisper of the Spirit Land, its wilderness and streams

A little time, another moon, the forests will be sad;
The streams will mourn the pleasant light that made their
    journeys glad;
The moon will faintly lighten up the sun light glisten cold
And wane into the western sky without the autumn gold.

And yet, I weep not for the sign of desolation near;

The ruin of my hunted race may only ask a tear
The wailing streams will laugh again, the naked trees put on
The beauty of their summer green beneath the summer sun.

The morning clouds will yet again their crimson draperies fold,
The star of sunset smile once more, a diamond set in gold;
But never for the forest path, or for the mountain's breath,
The mighty of our race shall leave the hunting ground of death.

I know the tale our fathers told, the legend of our fame,
The story of our spotless race before the "pale ones" came
When, asking fellowship with none, by turns the foe of all,
With ocean rearing up around its dark eternal wall

Compassionless and terrible our warriors stood alone.
And from the Big Lake to the sea the green earth was their own.
Where are they now? Around the changed and stranger peopled isle
A thousand graves are strewn beneath the mournful autumn smile;
The bow of strength is buried with the calumet and spear,
And the spent arrow slumbereth, forgetful of the deer.

The last canoe is rotting by the lake it glided o'er.
The footprints of the hunter race from all the hills are gone,
Their offering to the Spirit Land has left the altar stone.
The ashes of the council fire have no abiding token,
The song of war hath died away—the Powwah's charm is broken.

The startling warhoop cometh not upon the loud clear air;

The ancient woods are vanishing; the pale ones gather there.

And who is left to mourn for this? A solitary one,

Whose life is waning into death, like yonder sinking sun.

A broken reed—a blighted flower—that lingereth still behind

To mourn its faded sisterhood and wrestle with the wind.

Lo', from the Spirit Land I hear the music of the blest;

The holy faces of the loved are beaming from the west;

A voice is on the autumn winds—it calleth me away

Ere the cheek has lost its freshness and the raven tress is gray;

Ere the weight of years hath bowed me or the sunny eye is dim;

The father of my people is calling me to him.

Cormack's Business in St. John's

While Cormack's sales of foodstuff may originally have flourished, by the time he became involved in looking for the remnants of the Beothuk, his business had begun to deteriorate. During 1827 and 1828, advertisements in *The Royal Gazette* and *The Public Ledger* attest to the fact that Cormack & Co. continued with consignment sales, but Cormack had changed from items of food to dry goods, presumably hoping to entice new customers.[231] In May 1827, clothes, woollens, hosiery, cottons, silks, and linen, together with other goods "suitable for spring," were advertised for sale, but the articles he had chosen did not seem to be popular.[232] A few months later, he reverted to food items, with 400 bags of Hamburgh Bread, 100 barrels of Hamburgh flour, barrels of pork, and red wine being auctioned on Cormack's premises, including fabrics, rugs, mitts, fox traps, and more.[233]

It appears that the articles Cormack had chosen were not of interest to previous or new customers. Listed in the final auctions of goods that had not sold were flushing great coats and jackets, fancy waist coating, silk plaids, gentlemen's and ladies' silk stockings and kid gloves, crepe dresses and scarves, comforters, as well as a handsome grate, brass front, set of fire irons, complete kitchen oven, boxes of window glass, and ironmongery.[234] Cormack would have had little experience in this type of business and his choice of silk clothing, for example, may not have been prudent. He would also have lacked business connections. His repeated visits to Scotland and his search for Beothuk survivors, which kept him away from St. John's for several months at a time, would have had a detrimental effect on his status as an established St. John's merchant. Thompson, who may have held the business together, withdrew from the partnership with Cormack in 1828.[235] He subsequently pursued his own business and did well, but it accelerated Cormack's insolvency.

As planned, Cormack nevertheless left the country on January 14, 1828,[236] to lay his report on the Boeothick Institution before Earl Bathurst and give the Beothuk artifacts he had collected to Professor Jameson in Edinburgh. Upon his return to St. John's in May, he advertised for rent the waterfront premises of Roope's Plantation "at present occupied by the subscriber." They included for immediate possession "an excellent wharf, good stores, a comfortable Dwelling House, and every other convenience suitable for carrying on a large business"[237] (he would have offered a third of the property since his siblings still owned the other two-thirds). Also, two days were set aside that month for auctioning off a long list of goods at Cormack's shop.[238] In May and June, "Edinburgh Ale of very superior quality" was offered for sale, presumably in the expectation that it would sell as well as other food items had, and in September, J. Clift auctioned bread, tobacco, and snuff.[239]

On January 22, 1829, shortly after Shanawdithit had been transferred to the Simms household, Cormack sailed on the brig *Helen* for Greenock, never to return to Newfoundland.[240] In May, his business was declared insolvent,[241] and R.R. Wakeham and H. Hawson were appointed provisional trustees of the estate.[242] New efforts were made to rent out the waterfront premises[243] and, on May 8, an auction took place at which "all stock in trade, consisting of shop and store goods and household furniture" were offered for sale. Also in May, a sheriff's sale to satisfy a suit by James and Wm. Stewart against Cormack included furniture and household items, presumably from Cormack's dwelling.[244] In June, all remaining stock was sold by auction every Thursday and Saturday "until the whole [was] disposed of. By order of the Provisional Trustees of Wm. E. Cormack."[245] Later in the year, the provisional trustees were replaced by Edward Blake and James Stewart.[246] In September, a financial setback occurred when the *Seven Sisters* was lost at sea.[247] In that year, Cormack also sold his properties in Prince Edward Island, including one town lot and two half town lots in Charlottetown, and two large pasture lots, the second one 72 acres in total, as well as 5 acres of land at the head of Rustico Bay.[248]

The liquidation of Cormack's assets in St. John's dragged on for another two years. In May 1830, "all the right, title and interest of William E. Cormack, Insolvent, in those extensive and desirable waterside Premises and Land in this town—the interest of the Insolvent consists of one undivided third part of the said Premises"— were offered for sale.[249] On September 4, Cormack's share of the River Head Farm was purchased by David Stuart and James Gower Rennie as "executed by the Trustees of W.E. Cormack."[250] In July 1831, Cormack's creditors were requested to make their claims and to meet at the office of the subscriber "when a statement of the estate [would] be exhibited, and a dividend of the funds declared."[251]

Cormack was not entirely without financial support at that time. Eight lots with six houses and four shops[252] were still part of the Janet Cormack estate that continued to benefit all three of the Cormack children.[253] However, eventually both William Eppes and John Bell Cormack sold their one-third share of this part of the Roope's premises to D.S. Rennie. While Janet Grace Scott still owned one-third of Roope's, the transactions of William Eppes and John Bell would most likely have led to the creation of the "Scott and D.S. Rennie Estate," probably a trust, as marked on *The Plan of St. John's*.[254]

John Bell Cormack had run into financial difficulties in 1832 when he left Edinburgh "in haste" after the birth of his daughter, Anna Janet, in January 1831[255] and his marriage to Mary Ann Crawfuird, in April 1832.[256] In his letters to his stepbrother, David Stuart Rennie,[257] who worked in his law firm,[258] John Bell thanked him for sorting out his affairs and trying to secure money owed to him. John Bell also told him that he wanted to leave the country altogether and move to Prince Edward Island and that to do so he needed £250. Rennie appears to have accepted ownership of John Bell's shares in Roope's Plantation, including the building lots that were originally part of it, in exchange for a loan of the money.[259] John Bell and his family moved to Prince Edward Island in 1833. Rennie bought James Gower's part of the River Head Farm in 1833 (together, they had purchased W.E. Cormack's share in 1830), and presumably at that time or earlier W.E. Cormack also sold his share of Roope's Plantation to his stepbrother, David Stuart Rennie.

In 1836, John Bell Cormack was admitted a "Barrister and Solicitor of the Supreme Court" of Prince Edward Island[260] and his step-siblings subsequently gave him the power of attorney to represent their interests in that province.[261] He kept his shares in the River Head Farm and the property in the Victoria Park area (originally owned by his father) until 1848/1849.[262] Eventually, John Bell and his wife separated; his wife and their seven children moved to Boston, while John Bell stayed in Prince Edward Island and later returned to St. John's, where he died in 1869.[263]

Cormack Moves to London and Other Maritime Provinces

Cormack arrived in London in 1829 hoping to obtain employment in the British government service. To that end, he submitted several documents to Sir George Murray, Secretary of State for the Colonies, and requested an interview. Among the documents was his extensively researched paper "On the Political and Commercial Value of the Newfoundland, French, and North American Fishery" which he had written in the 1820s while he was still living in Newfoundland and which disclosed his remarkable knowledge about the fisheries in these areas. But it probably also disclosed Cormack's tendency to criticize government for its failure to utilize important resources. When he did not receive a positive response from Murray, he offered "to cross and explore New Holland and New South Wales [in Australia] in any direction."[264] Though Murray eventually granted Cormack an interview, this did not lead to the hoped-for government position.[265]

Without a job in England, Cormack moved to Prince Edward Island, where he established an export trade of grain to Britain.[266] He also continued with his research and writing. In early 1831, he sent his "Fisheries Paper" to the Natural History Society in Montreal. The manuscript was read to the Society on April 15, 1831, and won an essay competition,[267] with the proviso that Cormack give his permission to "the Society … to expunge certain passages of a warm political bearing, and which, as a literary Society, devoted solely to the advancement of knowledge, they cannot sanction by their approbation."[268] Cormack agreed, and received the prize that had been set out for the competition. It was most likely Cormack's criticism of Newfoundland's government for its neglect of the island's fisheries and Cormack's lack of discretion during the interview that had caused Murray to withhold a job offer, even though Cormack would have been well suited for the position. However, Murray sent the paper to the Board of Trade, presumably to seek the opinion of experts in the field about its value.[269]

In 1832/1833, Cormack submitted a considerably longer report of his trek in 1822 than the one published in 1824[270] to the Natural History Society of Montreal. It consists of 60 closely handwritten folio pages with a cover entitled "Narrative of a Journey across Newfoundland by W.E. Cormack (For the Natural History Society of Montreal)."[271] The original of this narrative is preserved in the McCord Museum archive. Although it is not the original field diary, it is written in that format.

One notable addition to this longer version is extensive information on the flora of Central Eastern Newfoundland, including the colour of flowering plants that do not bloom during late fall when Cormack had travelled across the island.[272] In 1823, Cormack's lack of information on plants was confirmed by a letter from Robert Morison, assistant surgeon of HMS *Sir Francis Drake* and an avid botanist, to Sir William Hooker at the Royal Botanic Gardens, Kew: "The few plants that W. Cormack took home [to Britain] from here [Newfoundland] I saw and named for him."[273] Cormack later told Hooker that Morison had "the best collection [of plants] that has been made in this quarter"[274] and urged him "to obtain the plants of our alpine district if they may be so called, at the Southwest and Northwest parts of the Island and of the Interior for there are plants not to be found nearer the Sea Coast. I only saw a little of these districts in 1822 and did not or rather could not examine their plants."[275] As it was, Hooker had already received a "hortus siccus" of Newfoundland plants from Morison.[276]

After Morison died, during Clapperton's exploration of Central Africa in December 1825, Cormack would have been able to gain access to Morison's plant collection, particularly as he was acquainted with Sir William Hooker,[277] who was a neighbour of the Rennies on Bath Street in Glasgow.[278] It has been suggested that Cormack included the names of many plants in Morison's collection, mostly in footnotes, in his manuscript for the Natural History Society. But while he may have profited from studying Morison's collection, his description of Newfoundland plants in the various biozones in his "Narrative of a Journey" was likely based on knowledge he had accumulated in the years following his trek.

Cormack continued with his interest in Newfoundland's flora and sent plants, collected in the vicinity of St. John's, to the Linnean Society in Britain.[279] Twenty-one plant specimens included in a list of vascular plants from Newfoundland in the Herbarium at the Royal Botanic Gardens in Kew are also noted as having come from Cormack,[280] and two specimens in the Grey Herbarium, also known as the Harvard University Herbarium, are listed as "collected by Cormack in Newfoundland between 1822 and 1829."[281]

Sometime in the 1830s, Cormack moved to Cape Breton.[282] It is likely that he became involved with the General Mining Association in Cape Breton Island, for he later claimed to have been "connected somewhat extensively with the opening and active management of coal mines."[283] Another of Cormack's activities was that of agent for the New Brunswick and Nova Scotia Land Company,[284] and in 1833 he became a citizen of Fredericton, New Brunswick.[285] During the winter of 1833/1834, Cormack went to Britain to consult with various parties on behalf of the Land Company and returned to Fredericton in 1834.[286] But when he clashed with W. Kendal, another agent of the Land Company, both men had to present their case to the Board of Directors in London. The Board agreed with Kendal's argument, and Cormack left the company.

Cormack Moves to Australia in 1836

In the wake of this setback, Cormack emigrated to Australia.[287] Much of the description of Cormack's years in Australia, New Zealand, and British Columbia is based on Bernard Fardy's *William Epps Cormack, Newfoundland Pioneer,* 1985.[288]

On May 7, 1836, Cormack boarded the barque *Clarinda* as the general cargo ship's solitary passenger for a journey of 12,000 miles to Sydney, Australia. The *Clarinda* arrived there on September 14, after almost four months at sea.[289] When Cormack began to look for some means of livelihood, an acquaintance from one of the Atlantic provinces suggested that he apply for the job of Clerk to the Bench of Petty Sessions Court at Dungog. Cormack followed this advice and in 1837 took up his duties at Dungog, a flourishing farming district about 70 miles north of Sydney. His annual salary was £100, but with this job came the added duties of Postmaster of the district, which paid him an additional £10 per year.

In the beginning, Cormack's duties went well, and he performed them efficiently. Some months after he had started his two jobs, the postal district of Dungog was amalgamated with that of Port Stephens, about 30 miles to the southeast. As Dungog was the central town of the district, Cormack was required to be in the Dungog post office four days a week to take care of the mail and to travel to the post office at Port Stephens once every two weeks.[290] His court duties were performed at Stroud, 20 miles east of Dungog. Between the two centres and his two jobs, Cormack would have found the pace of the required travel hectic.

His job as court clerk at Stroud often caused him to be away when the mail arrived at the Dungog post office. His absence either resulted in a delay in opening the mail or the mail was opened and handed out by an official of the Police Magistrate's office. The Police Magistrate, Thomas Cook, resented having to take on what he rightfully believed to be Cormack's responsibilities. Within a year, an animosity developed between the two men, which turned into a running feud over the next few years. Eventually, Cook complained to Cormack's supervisor, Postmaster General Raymond, in Sydney.

Cook complained about Cormack's laxity in performing his duties and made it plain that he was irked by the fact that he or his constables were often compelled to do the work that Cormack was being paid to do. In Cook's opinion, Cormack felt it "beneath the dignity of a Clerk to the Court of Petty Sessions to do so."[291] He suggested that Cormack might operate more efficiently by having certain hours on particular days in which to be available for his jobs.

Raymond investigated the complaints against Cormack and found them to be valid. But his reprimands to Cormack were not taken kindly. Cormack informed his boss what he thought of Cook's complaints and Raymond's admonitions. He found the duties of postmaster of Dungog "mechanical" and felt that they had been "palmed on him" by the colonial government. It was a penny-pinching move and was too much for one man to handle, considering the travel involved. He thought that the situation was a "disgrace to the government and an insult to common sense and the people for whose benefit the office was established."[292]

The tense situation at Dungog continued. Raymond took his frustrations directly to the governor of New South Wales, Sir George Gipps, whose remonstrances, he hoped, would intimidate Cormack. He was fair, however, in noting that he could find no one to assume the duties of postmaster for the paltry salary of £10.[293] But even Gipp's warnings to Cormack had no effect. Cormack was adamant that the two jobs could not be handled by one man. As Cook's complaints continued, Raymond suggested to Gipps that Cormack's pay as court clerk and as postmaster be impounded until Cormack posted his bond, a requirement that had been overlooked when Cormack took on the jobs. But when Cormack received no pay, he resigned from both his positions.

After some search, Cormack leased a farm named East Bank on the banks of the William's River at a place called Croompark, a few miles from Dungog. To make a success of his newest venture, Cormack needed labour, and in Australia in the 1830s that meant convict servants. The law allowed any freeman who ventured into any enterprise that would develop and benefit the colonies to apply to the colonial government for the required number of convicts to be used as labourers to help him pursue his goal. Cormack applied to Gipps, and notwithstanding Gipp's dislike for the volatile Scotsman, he awarded him the custody of five lads, aged 14 to 21, who had been sent to the Australian colony to serve out their sentences for crimes they had committed in England.[294] Cormack chose to grow tobacco, which was a relatively new idea on the Australian continent, and he was one of the first to cultivate it commercially.[295] His innovative effort went well for a year but even in this remote and peaceful location, Cook found a way to make Cormack's life miserable.

On the morning of April 17, 1839, John Parnell, one of Cook's constables, happened upon Cormack's farm. He had a prisoner in tow, shackled and under the gun. The two men were dripping from a night in the bush during heavy rain. They were looking for a place to cross the nearby river on their way to Dungog. But it was swollen with flooding and this is when the two men came upon Cormack's farm. Cormack invited them to his carpenter's house, where they could dry their clothes and get some food from the carpenter's wife. He also told them that he would give them food and provisions to see them over their stay at his farm while they waited for the river to drop enough for them to cross. He also suggested that they might work for their food on his fields. But a few hours later Parnell told Cormack that he was going to cross the river and continue on to Dungog. Cormack warned him that he would have to leave his gun behind and take off the prisoner's shackles and once he was on the other side, he had no way of controlling him. In fact, if the prisoner was a good swimmer, he might escape.

Despite Cormack's warning, Parnell crossed the river and later placed a complaint charging that Cormack had "turned him off his farm and ill used him and thus forced him to swim across the river." Most likely he lost his prisoner in the process and was now looking for an excuse. Cormack was summoned to appear in court on May 21 to answer the charge. But he submitted his own affidavit accusing Parnell of perjury.[296] He also asked Gipps[297] to intercede on his behalf, something Gipps would not do. While Cook was delighted that Gipps would not support Cormack, when the case came up before Magistrate J.P. Ellsworth in Dungog, it was thrown out, because Parnell had again been dismissed from his post as Constabulary Officer.

Cormack Moves to New Zealand in 1839

Disgusted by Gipp's government and corrupt officials such as Cook, Cormack began thinking about moving to some place as yet not under British colonial rule. The islands of New Zealand, some 1,200 miles east of Australia, seemed promising. It was still a no-man's land politically and, although no European country had yet laid claim to it, the French were quite active, especially on the South Island, while the British had the greatest number of settlers on the North Island. Meanwhile, the British government had become concerned about the lawlessness among the settlers and, at least overtly, the exploitation of the Maori, who often returned violence for violence. England was also worried that if she did not move quickly to assert authority over the islands, France would.[298]

From his influential friends in England, Cormack learned that Britain was, indeed, about to claim the New Zealand islands by making a treaty with the Maori. With British possession would come an influx of settlers who would require land. Hence, Cormack embarked on the career of a real estate agent. Back home in England, men of means were interested in his scheme, and he was engaged by three of them to purchase land for them, and for himself, which could later be sold to land-hungry settlers.

As the New Zealand Company, founded by E.G. Wakefield, was already buying up much land from the Maori in the southern part of the North Island,[299] Cormack headed to the northern part, to the fertile valleys of the Waikato and Waipa rivers. From October 1839 to February 1840, he travelled the countryside buying up land from the Maori. Some of this land was signed over to him in exchange for goods, including guns and ammunition that the Maori coveted.[300] He eventually laid claim, for himself and others, to more than 42,000 acres of prime farming and pastoral land.[301] Very shortly afterward, the Royal Navy, under Captain William Hobson, arrived, and Hobson immediately began travelling around the island selling the Maori a treaty. Hobson used the church missionaries, who had been present in New Zealand for 25 years, as his agents. Although these agents had met with little success in Christianizing the Indigenous population, they had power and influence with both the Maori and the British government. From all accounts, they did a good job, for in the words of one New Zealand historian, Hobson's agents successfully "hawked the treaty throughout the major North Island tribes."[302]

The Treaty of Waitangi, as it is known to history, was signed on February 6, 1840, between the British government and some Maori groups. It was more of an agreement than an official cession of lands by the Maori, as far as the Maori were concerned. However, the British government presented it as a pact whereby they would deal exclusively with the Maori to guard their welfare and protect their rights, when in reality the British regarded the treaty as their official right to make New Zealand a Crown colony.

Cormack saw Governor Gipps of New South Wales (Australia) as the treaty's main supporter, for it was into his hands that the reins of power would fall once the islands became a Crown colony. He blamed Gipps for the acceptance of the treaty by the Maori as it was "hurriedly obtained by means of false statements, persuasion and bribery on the part of the representatives of her Majesty."[303] The Maori signed the treaty, Cormack believed, not knowing—as did the white settlers—that a British governor was already on the islands and that the English intended to turn the islands into a Crown colony.

For months afterwards, the document of the treaty was circulated through the islands. The agents, that is, the missionaries, "most of whom" as Cormack put it, were "of a very low order, who understood the Maori language and helped to mislead the chiefs."[304] Hobson became the first governor of the new colony and was manipulated by Gipps from New South Wales for a year before the islands became a separate colony of the British Empire. Hobson could only adhere to the philosophy of the acrimonious governor, who believed that "savages have no right to the soil they happen to be discovered upon by Europeans."[305]

The Treaty of Waitangi provided that all lands were to be Crown owned and could only be granted or sold by the government. For independent landowners such as Cormack and his partners, this stipulation of the treaty was to cause everlasting hardship. Cormack let the British takeover settle and went back to Australia to continue farming. Raising tobacco had proven to be profitable, and he again leased the 320-acre farm at East Bank from its owner, John Hook Went. In March 1841, he returned to Croompark and found himself facing his old rival Thomas Cook. Cook had dug up another charge against Cormack and this time set out to make it stick. He extracted from two of Cormack's servants' statements that said that Cormack had, two years earlier, appropriated and kept some property of Cook's, valued at £10. Cormack was promptly served with Cook's charges and the sworn affidavits of his two servants. One of them had been due to have his "ticket of leave" come up for review at which time it was up to Cook to decide whether he was to remain a servant in some relatively easy employ or be sent back to prison. Cormack claimed that Cook used this situation to coerce the men into saying what he wanted. They later admitted that they had lied, and Cormack's other servants backed their master's innocence.

Cormack asked Gipps for assistance, reminding him that in the Parnell affair he had done him an injustice and claiming that Cook was covetous of his property and wanted to see him arrested and out of the way.[306] Gipps nevertheless refused to support him. Cormack left the farm at East Bank under the care of his servants and left for New Zealand.

In spring 1842, he boarded a ship for New Zealand sailing to the fledgling settlement of Auckland in Commercial Bay on the North Island where he could be near his land claims in the Waikato and Waipa valleys.[307] He purchased a 22-ton schooner, *Roory O'More,* to trade oil and whalebone.[308] The new colony had meanwhile been given status independent of New South Wales. While the new administration settled in at Auckland, Cormack opened a watchmaker's shop on Shortland Street, the busy waterfront thoroughfare of the frontier town.[309]

Cormack found that during his short absence the land controversy had grown even more uncertain. The New Zealand Company had purchased huge tracts of land in the southern portion of the North Island and the Crown had taken over administration of the lands in the northern part. A new Land Claim Act retroactively required all land purchases from the Maori to be approved by a British Land Commission. Thus, Cormack suddenly found that all his claims had still to be approved.[310]

As settlers were looking to government lands in the north, Cormack was willing to sell some of the land to interested persons who would repay him his investment and agree to pay the Maori the balance of the trade goods he had promised them to complete the transaction.[311] However, the Crown Lands Commissioner, Donald McLean, would not allow Cormack to do this, claiming that he had no knowledge of settlers wanting to purchase land. Cormack seems to have believed that McLean was holding out to have all of Cormack's land claims rescinded.

Cormack Travels to London in 1843

Perturbed by the fact that his claims were not dealt with, Cormack decided, in 1843, to travel to England to inform his partners of the situation. He stopped over in Sydney and arranged to dispose of his interests in Australia. He sold the unexpired term of his lease on East Bank to one John McKay for 10 shillings and signed over to him his rights to the convict servants.[312]

In London, he appraised his partner, Henry H. Willis, and other investors[313] of the developments in New Zealand and secured an ally in his attempts to influence British Parliament: an old school friend, the Marquis of Breadalbane. Cormack reiterated to him the fraudulence of the Treaty of Waitangi and condemned the new Land Claim Act, which retroactively required all land purchases from the Maori to be approved by a British Land Commission[314] and was thereby "sweeping away at once their capital and their credit."[315] Cormack may also have found a sympathetic ear with his old friend, John MacGregor, who was now Secretary of the Board of Trade to the Colonies.

While in London, Cormack stayed with Mr. Willis at Crosby Square[316] and at this time wrote or rewrote his history "Of the Red Indians of Newfoundland," including the stories told by Shanawdithit, and also his "Geology and Mineralogy" of Newfoundland, as both these manuscripts were written on paper with the watermarks 1840 and 1843.[317] Most likely, Cormack had left his material on Newfoundland matters, collected in the 1820s, with his partner Willis before he had set off for Australia in 1836.

During his sojourn in London Cormack met Michael Faraday and part of a conversation with him about his experiences in Newfoundland was published in *The Correspondence of Michael Faraday*.[318]

Cormack Returns to New Zealand

Satisfied that he had done all he could to advise those interested in the developments in the newest colony, and feeling that he had some revitalized support, Cormack returned to New Zealand and found that things had changed a little for the better. Hobson had died and was replaced by Captain Fitzroy. Because Fitzroy had little funding to combat the warring Maori in the south of the island, dealing with the land question had ground to a halt. He relaxed the regulation that only the Crown could buy land from the Maori, which would have led Cormack to expect that at least his disputed claims would be settled. But Fitzroy was soon replaced by Earl George Grey, who immediately reinstated the government monopoly on buying and selling land. Shrewd and tough, Grey also was ruthless in dealing with the rebellious Maori bands; he kidnapped a Maori chief and several sub-chiefs and held them in captivity until he had assurances that the violence would end.

Under Grey's governance, Cormack could make no headway in settling his land claims. Two years earlier his claims had been intensely investigated at hearings at the district court of Auckland held by the "Chief Protector," George Clarke. Evidence had been heard from several Maori chiefs and their sworn depositions were taken. Some claimed to have sold the land to Cormack and had been paid fairly for it. Others said that they had not agreed to the sales. Backed by the supporting chiefs and the translator who had acted for him at the transactions, Cormack proved to the satisfaction of the "Chief Protector" that he had legally bought and paid for the lands he claimed. Still, despite his proof, no grants were issued to him by the Crown.[319] He had purchased for himself and his partners land intending to go into large-scale horse and cattle ranching. But by 1846, Cormack had given up this plan as not being feasible.[320]

Meanwhile, Cormack proceeded with setting up a small sawmill on one of his parcels of land in the Waipa River valley and obtained a contract with the British Admiralty to supply them with spars from the long and strong Kuari or Cowrie pine. He used Maori labour to procure the spars and handed over the mill to them in payment for their efforts.[321] Colonial officials, however, warned him that his supply of wood might lead to legal action since the trees might be coming from lands which the Maori had already ceded to the Crown.[322]

As the Cowrie pine was probably the best suited tree to use for spars, Cormack thought that they might be grown in England. He therefore sent specimens of the tree's seeds to his botanical friends at Kew Gardens for study and observation. But the seeds never arrived, and Cormack was ever after under the impression that something underhanded had happened to them.

One of Cormack's interests had been the British judicial system and in 1845 he sought and received an appointment as Justice of the Peace for the Auckland district.[323] He took up the case of English merchants who had already been trying for three and a half years to receive compensation for property of theirs which had been seized by government officials upon the death of their agent. The case became quite controversial in England while, in New Zealand, Cormack feared that it would never be settled. He wrote to the governor, expressing concern about his lack of action, which would make it appear "that there is no security for property in New Zealand," a fact that would deter willing capitalists from investing in property in this country.[324]

In 1845, news reached New Zealand that the British government was about to pass an act that would set up a Legislative Council in the colony. Cormack would have been delighted and expressed his intention to seek a seat on the council. The act was passed in Parliament in 1846 but Grey blatantly refused to invoke it.[325]

Eventually, most of Cormack's land purchases were disallowed,[326] a decision he disputed unsuccessfully.[327] Disillusioned by the political machinations of Grey, by the treatment of the Maori and the injustices shown to the first settlers, Cormack appears to have admitted defeat. Despite all his efforts, the support he had counted on in England was not as influential as he had expected. Clearly, New Zealand was not working out for him and, in the spring of 1849, he boarded the brig *Dorset* and sailed for England.

Cormack Returns to London

On his travel to England, Cormack brought with him a plant collection for Professor Hooker that was, unfortunately, spoiled on arrival when the glass cover of the case was broken. Only a kauri seedling survived.[328] While in New Zealand, Cormack had also obtained a Moa bone, which he asked his nephew George, the son of his sister, Janet Grace, to deliver to Professor Richard Owen, conservator at the Hunterian Museum, who published a photograph of it and Cormack's description of the "Locality of the remains of the *Dinornis Giganteus*" in his *Memoirs on the Extinct Wingless Birds of New Zealand*[329] (Appendix 2). (According to Owen, the specimen was actually *Dinornis gracilis*.) Guided by a Maori, Cormack had found the bone on the northern part of the island, on a cliff above Opito Bay, next to an old Maori fireplace that was buried under 3 feet of sandy soil.

While in London, Cormack took on another project, revising a booklet on ice-skating, a sport at which he excelled.[330] He called it *The Art of Skating Practically Explained by Lieut. R. Jones, R.D. with Revisions and Additions by W.E. Cormack, Esq. (1855)*,[331] which was based on Robert Jones's 1772 *A Treatise on Skating*.[332] Cormack extended the text, added instructions for more complex figures on the ice, gave directions for the construction of skates, and for different methods of affixing them to the foot. He added new drawings of skaters in the outfits of the day, all male.[333] Cormack also used his time in London to burnish "with Dr. [Andrew] Ure and others his old Scotch lore in Metallurgy-Mineralogy etc."[334]

In June 1851, Newfoundland's Surveyor General, Joseph Noad, had tracked Cormack down and communicated to him his interest in the Beothuk and his intention to present a lecture on this subject. Cormack generously let him have his material on the Beothuk, which he had kept all these years, probably at the Willis's house in London, at Crosby Square. It included Shanawdithit's lengthy story of the last years of her people, his own "History of the Red Indians of Newfoundland," pages from his letter book, records of the Boeothick Institution, artifacts, a vocabulary, and various notes.[335] J.P. Howley, who became an authority on the Beothuk, and published this material in *The Beothucks or Red Indians,* in 1915, called some of the notes "Stray Notes in Cormack's handwriting such as titles of drawings, of Beothuk songs and customs, the story of Shanawdithit being shot at, and the location of the vocabulary of the Red Indians. They also listed artifacts he was giving to Noad, such as birch rind culinary vessels, birch rind canoes, spear point and drawings by Shanawdithit; a map of the interior, the Narrative of my journey in search of the aborigines. (in ms.)." (This was the account of his trek across the island in 1822.) The notes were signed "W.E. Cormack, 24th June 1851,"[336] which appears to have been the date Cormack accumulated the material for Noad, shortly before he left for California.

Noad included Cormack's information in his lecture to the Mechanic's Institute which he presented in January 1853 to a "numerous and respectable audience."[337] It was published by *The Patriot Press* in the same year.[338] Noad also recognized that Cormack's narrative of his trek across the island in 1822—a longer and more polished version than the one he had sent to the Natural History Society in Montreal, with the plant names incorporated into the text—was a valuable record and recommended to Governor Charles H. Darling to have it published. In 1856, at government expense, *The Morning Post* and the *Commercial Journal* printed the *Narrative of a Journey across the Island of Newfoundland by W E. Cormack, Esq. The Only One Ever Performed by a European.*[339] On leaving the province in 1855, Noad placed the box with Cormack's papers in the library of the Atheneum-Mechanic's Institute.

Cormack Travels to California during the Gold Rush, 1851–1858

After two years in London, for all indications with no employment, Cormack emigrated in the wake of a gold rush to California, where political developments were to his liking.[340] He travelled by sea via New York to Panama and from there through the Panama Canal and then on the SS *California* to San Francisco, arriving on October 5, 1851.[341] At the time, San Francisco was one of the fastest growing cities. On average, 30 houses were built per day and the harbour was crowded with ships jammed side to side.

Cormack went into business with the merchant M.W. Cromartie, who operated a mercantile establishment under the name of Smith & Bros. at the northwest corner of California and Battery streets.[342] During the gold rush years, San Francisco was a merchant's paradise. Prices were exorbitant. A dozen eggs sold for as high as $6.[343] With such prices, merchants could not afford to be too selective about the cargoes they bought. Whole shipments, which were often auctioned off at the wharves or in the middle of the street, had to be purchased by the merchants just so they could get the commodity they wanted. The remainder would simply be left for the taking.

San Francisco and the "wild west" were a far cry from the frontiers Cormack had pioneered in other parts of the world. Along with its unprecedented prosperity, the city had unprecedented lawlessness. Large gangs of rowdies regularly prowled the streets, robbing and assaulting citizens. One of the most infamous of these gangs was the "Sydney Ducks," who operated from a shacktown ghetto of the city known as "Sydney town." They were men from the rugged frontier settlements of Australia and New Zealand who had embarked to the California gold rush from Sydney, Australia. Many were escaped prisoners or bond labourers of the type Cormack had employed on his farm at East Bank and were in the country illegally. To control these gangs, more civic-minded people of the town formed a Committee of Vigilance to combat their lawlessness. They quickly grew powerful, were greatly feared, and highly effective.

By 1854, San Francisco experienced a decrease in prosperity. Prices suddenly dropped and labour moved away, and 300 merchants went out of business. Smith & Bros., however, remained solvent.[344] In January 1855, Cormack held a job as postmaster in O'Byrnes Ferry, Calaveras County, and from 1856 to 1858 he is listed in the San Francisco city directories as a merchant living at 118 Sacramento Street.[345]

During these years of up and down prosperity and tenuous survival, Cormack varied the mundane chores of the mercantile world with his special interest in botany. He formed a *hortus siccus* of the exotic and varied plants of the state of California, collecting unusual specimens of plants and sending them to the famed Linnean Society of England.[346] One of his specimens, a common heath, was the subject of long discussions in the Society as to whether it was native to the American continent.[347]

By 1856, more mechanized mining techniques had greatly improved the industry, and progress returned to the stagnating city of

San Francisco. The big boom had peaked and over the next few years the city began to lose some of its liveliness. As serenity settled over the city, Cormack may have felt that the challenge of California had been met, and it seems that he looked for yet another one. In the spring of 1858, word reached San Francisco of a new gold strike on the Fraser River in British Columbia. Although, eight years earlier, Cormack had said that he would never again live in a British colony, the lure of a new horizon seems to have been too much for him to resist.

Cormack Moves to British Columbia in 1859

Late in January 1859, Cormack arrived in Victoria, British Columbia, and, on the first of February, wrote to Governor James Douglas offering his services. He forwarded letters of introduction from William Lane Booker, British Consul in San Francisco, and from his former partner, Cromartie, who highly recommended him as a "Scotsman of education" and "a man of moral worth and energy of character."[348] Douglas was impressed by Cormack's references and resumé and before the month was out, Cormack was working as the governor's secretary. At first, and contrary to his previous experience, it appeared that he was intending to settle in British Columbia. As he put it, "my employment here in a public capacity is likely to be of a permanent measure."[349] He applied for a piece of land in New Westminster on which to build a house, since certain lots were reserved for government officials as they were considered to be "of no commercial value."[350]

For close to two years, Cormack remained with his secretarial duties. But gradually, he recognized the shortcomings of this British colony and his desire for a more just government would have stirred again. He became acquainted with William Alexander Smith, better known as Amor de Cosmos, who had lately made his way from Nova Scotia via the California gold fields to New Westminster. De Cosmos, a political activist, wanted to emulate his home province hero, Joseph Howe, who had led the fight for representative government in Nova Scotia.[351] Immediately upon his arrival in the colony, de Cosmos launched his campaign to win representative government for British Columbia and started a small newspaper in New Westminster which he used as his mouthpiece to attack Douglas's administration.

During 1859/1860, one of his regular columnists was W.E. Cormack. In his position as secretary to the governor, Cormack could not vent any of his political views, especially those that were in favour of abolishing his boss's job. His essays and articles therefore consisted primarily of discourses on the fishery of Newfoundland and the parallel potentials of those in British Columbia. De Cosmos viewed Cormack's innovative ideas as a means of promoting his own ends. On one of Cormack's articles on the British Columbian fishery, he wrote: "We view it as a duty on the part of the government to foster by every rational means our fishery and that it becomes the people to emulate the example of our hardy brethren in Newfoundland and the Lower Provinces, in their development."[352]

In January 1861, Cormack would have found that the colonial government of British Columbia was not much better than those he had encountered in other parts of the world. He left his position as secretary to sit on the first Municipal Council of New Westminster and, as its chairman, strongly advocated, as he had in New Zealand and Australia, representative government for British Columbia.[353] In January 1862, he was invited by Colonial Secretary W.A.G. Young to act as one of three judges of essays that were submitted to the government on the capabilities of the colony.[354] He was also invited to submit his ideas for the development of the fishery in British Columbia. To be asked about his ideas would have been a new experience for Cormack.

In response, he prepared a lengthy essay on the "Fisheries of North America," in which he expressed the view that not only the markets of Europe but also those of Australia and the far Pacific relied heavily on the fishery of the North Atlantic. He suggested that a fishery, developed on the west coast of North America, particularly in British Columbia, could eventually capture the markets of Australia, New Zealand, and the South Pacific.[355] He even outlined how that industry could be developed, using the example of the Newfoundland fishery and its system of granting "fishing-rooms" and bounties. As excited as he would have been about being asked for his opinion, he was probably not too surprised when his ideas were flatly rejected.[356]

To sustain himself, Cormack again turned his hand to mercantile pursuits, advertising a variety of clothing, hardware, liquor, tobacco, and other items "for sale by the undersigned at the store of A.R. Green," on the waterfront of New Westminster, presumably selling them on consignment under his name.[357]

Since his arrival in the colony, Cormack had found that the Indians were treated with the same lack of respect shown to the Maori of New Zealand and the Beothuk of Newfoundland and that they did not receive the justice they deserved. As was the case in Newfoundland and New Zealand, he was drawn to take up their cause. Impressed with the work of Father Fouquet, a Roman Catholic missionary working and living among the Indians near New Westminster, he wrote to the governor on behalf of the priest, requesting a piece of land "a lot in some retired part of town, or otherwise a portion of suburban land ... for the purpose of erecting a chapel for the Indians."[358] Although not a Roman Catholic—Cormack was probably a member of the Church of England—he showed that he was not affected with the narrow-minded bigotry so prevalent in his times and appreciated Fouquet's work for what it was worth.

And then an incident caused Cormack to become more vocally supportive. In January 1862, four "Whitemen," two of them armed, went to the Indian settlement of Koketlam, near New Westminster, to seek revenge for some alleged injustice done to them by the Indians. During the ensuing argument, they shot one of the Indians, who later died of his injuries. The two men who had been armed were held responsible and were brought up on charges before a Grand Jury but were acquitted of any wrongdoing. Cormack would have figured that the two were guilty of something, as a man had been killed. The case had been handled sloppily; there was no post-mortem and the investigation by the Grand Jury was cursory.[359]

Cormack believed that the unjust verdict was due to the presence of transient persons from England and elsewhere sitting on the Grand Jury, and he began a campaign to have Grand Juries abolished in the colony. He contacted influential men of the community and wrote letters to newspapers and other organizations that would publicize his cause. He wrote that the late Solicitor General, Sir Romelly, together with other legislators, had been decidedly in favour of doing away with Grand Juries or otherwise excluding foreigners from that power "obtaining a preponderating influence in our fundamental legislative institutions."[360]

While agitating for representative government and pressing to gain equality for the Indians, Cormack also prepared British Columbia's fishery exhibit to be included in the World Exhibition in London. His prize entry in the exhibit were sockeye salmon from the Fraser River, but the salmon never reached London. The fish had been shipped with their stomachs intact to permit ichthyological studies, but the salmon had spoiled during their transport and had to be discarded.[361]

In the winter of 1862 Cormack, age 66, delighted and astonished everybody by his graceful evolutions on the ice.[362] He was also credited with involvement in bringing young women from Britain to New Westminster for the purpose of providing marriage partners and/ or domestics.[363]

In 1863, Cormack was most likely gratified to see his efforts to win representative government for the colony realized. That year the colony acquired its first Legislative Council, and heading it was his old friend and editor, Amor de Cosmos. Cormack was elected to the Board of Management of the Royal Columbian Hospital and, on October 31, formed "The Agricultural Association of the District and City of New Westminster."[364] As secretary of the Association, he encouraged other districts and towns to form similar associations to promote "the great agricultural interests of the colony."[365] Cormack also began a correspondence with the Highland Society of Scotland and sent them grass seeds which he thought could be grown in that country. He also hit upon the unlikely scheme of introducing British Columbian mountain sheep into the highlands of Scotland with the intention of breeding them with Scottish sheep to improve the quality of wool in Great Britain.[366] British Columbians of the 1860s, however, were little interested in associations and institutions and Cormack's Agricultural Association had a rather languid and short-lived existence.

Encouraged by Father Fouquet, Cormack accepted the post of Superintendent of Indian Demonstrations for the district of New Westminster in 1864. Throughout the next two years, he was responsible for Indian celebrations, demonstrations, and visits to the town, at which gatherings the Indigenous people expected to receive gifts or, at least, have their room and board paid for by the colonial government. They were great revelers and Cormack singlehandedly had to organize the affairs, distribute the goods, and account for every expenditure, which meant that he had to scrupulously justify and account for every dollar spent on these occasions to the government.

Cormack also continued his agitation for the development of a fishery in the colony. In July 1864, he applied for a "Licence of Occupation for the purpose of carrying on the salmon or other fishery" in Barrard Inlet. He requested that the Licence of Occupation "continue valid until a law was made to regulate such matters in British Columbia."[367] But his application was turned down, the government official in charge suggested that they had "better wait until a law is made."

Worn out by his active life and journeys around the world, Cormack's health began to fail in his 70s. His ideas to promote and develop the colony of British Columbia had largely been met with resistance and he might have decided that his contributions had been enough. Alone and in ill health, he would have found that, for all his enterprise, he had no lasting financial support. Hence, when a public library was founded in New Westminster, he took on the job of chief librarian and immediately requested money from the government to defray the expenses of the library and to stock it with books and materials.[368]

Early in 1868, Cormack's health had deteriorated to the point that he could no longer perform his duties as librarian. No information is available about his ailment, but a friend of his who described Cormack's last months said that he experienced "great bodily suffering somewhat tinged with bitterness a temper which was constitutionally mild ... Though afflicted for years he was only confined to bed for about a month. His sufferings during the greater part of his confinement, though intense, never affected his mental powers. With a clear intellect and consolatory resignation he met the approach of Death."[369]

On April 29, 1868, six days before his 72nd birthday, William Eppes Cormack died. Practically the whole town of New Westminster turned out for his funeral. The fire department, of which he had recently been made an honorary member, acted as his pallbearers. The service was presided over by his long-time friend Father Fouquet, and he was laid to rest in the little cemetery of Holy Trinity Church on the Indian reservation in New Westminster—the lot of land Cormack had been instrumental in acquiring for the missionary and the Indigenous people.[370]

Cormack numbered among his friends or correspondents some of the most celebrated scientific and literary men of the 19th century, such as Sir William Hooker, Professor Richard Owen, Professor Faraday, Dr. Ure, Dr. Hodgkin (Chairman of the Aborigines Protection Society), Professor Jameson of the Edinburgh Museum, and John Macgregor, author of the *Progress of America, Commercial Statistics &c*, the last a particularly close friend. Newspaper reviews described Cormack in the following terms: "His warm appreciation of what he deemed the good works of the Roman Catholic Missionaries in this colony showed that he had no narrow-minded religious notions … While he sought the respectable gains of commerce, he at the same time aimed at extending international knowledge, thus contributing to the welfare and happiness of man."[371]

Cormack's Legacy in Newfoundland

In 1881, at the first meeting of the Newfoundland Historical Society at the Atheneum library, Reverend Moses Harvey reported that on that morning an old box with papers about the transactions of the Boeothick Institution and other documents had been found in the library. The box was placed into the hands of J.P. Howley, at that time assistant to Alexander Murray of the Geological and Topographical Survey of Newfoundland, who had developed a particular interest in the Beothuk. At a follow-up meeting of the society, Howley announced that the box contained "William Eppes Cormack's papers from his years in Newfoundland in the 1820s." He described its contents as "a history of the Beothuk, including the information provided by Shanawdithit, proceedings of the Boeothick Institution, correspondence of its members, reports about searches for Beothuk survivors, an old map (*Steel's Chart of Newfoundland*, 1817 used by Cormack on his trek across the island), five bark maps, and notes in Cormack's hand." Much of this material, including Cormack's report on his trek across Newfoundland in 1822, was later included in Howley's 1915 *The Beothucks or Red Indians*, published by Cambridge University Press.

In 1828, F.A. Bruton reprinted the report of Cormack's trek "for use in schools," with botanical names, a glossary, and other information neatly tucked into five appendices.[372] Hence, the story of Cormack and Sylvester's feat came to be standard fare in Newfoundland's school curriculum.[373]

Three years later, Ernest Cormack Finch, solicitor in Britain and grandson of Cormack's sister, Janet Grace Scott, sent a photograph which he believed to be that of W.E. Cormack to Robin J. Rennie of St. John's, grandson of William Frederick Rennie. A copy of this photograph (Figure 1) has found its way into the Legislature,[374] the Archive, and its Special Collections Division at Memorial University. It is the only known portrait of Cormack and has been widely reproduced.

Today, Newfoundlanders generally know about Cormack and Sylvester's trek across the island and appreciate their achievement; Cormack has also been celebrated by naming geographical features and places after him. A mountain west of Middle Ridge is called Mount Cormack and a lake north of King George VI Lake named Cormack's Lake.[375] A community in western Newfoundland was formally given the name Cormack.[376] A school, streets, a square, a bridge, and business establishments bear his name[377] and a 182-kilometre walking trail from St. George's Bay across the rugged Anguille Mountains to Petites on the south coast has been named Cormack Trail in his honour.[378] Cormack's guide, Joseph Sylvester, was honoured by Cormack when he named a mountain Mount Sylvester.[379]

Cormack and Sylvester's trek has also inspired attempts to walk or drive or ski Cormack's route. An extensively documented recreation of the trek, supported by *Canadian Geographic*, was undertaken by journalist Don Cayo and photographer Ray Fennelly in the fall of 1991.[380] Though they occasionally used roads, their route meshed with that of Cormack and Sylvester, hitting some of the same high spots.

The two men completed the journey in 39 days, travelling close to 600 kilometres. There were also three scouters of the 6th St. John's Troop who "followed in Cormack's steps" in 1960, walking largely on roads and railway beds.[381] Eight men from central Newfoundland crossed the island on skidoos in 1971. It took the party 12 days to reach St. George's Bay, and their odometers showed a distance of 568 kilometres.[382] In September 1994, the 27-person Assaults Pioneer Platoon from the Canadian Forces Base at Gagetown, New Brunswick, walked from Milton, Trinity Bay, to St. George's Bay as a personal endurance test.[383] And there were others.[384]

Over the years the cemetery of Holy Trinity Church in New Westminster, BC, where Cormack had been interred, was neglected and in the early 1940s was levelled to make room for a school.[385] When journalist Don Morris collected information on the whereabouts of Cormack's grave,[386] he discovered the gravestone. He sent a photograph of it to Newfoundland and presumably also to the town of New Westminster (Figure 10). As a result, a large, framed photograph of Cormack with a commemorative text was unveiled at New Westminster's City Hall and later moved to the museum of that town.[387] The inscription text states:

In memory of William Eppes Cormack, born May 5, 1796, St. John's, Newfoundland, died April 30 1868,[388] New Westminster, B.C. Explorer, Entrepreneur, Philanthropist, Agriculturist, Author. Whose name is honoured in the country of his birth for his expedition across the Island of Newfoundland in 1822, and for his unremitting efforts on behalf of the Beothuk Indians of the Colony and their traditions, AND his life by this plaque, erected in the city of his burial, for his services in the promotion of the City of New Westminster, the Colony of British Columbia, and the enrichment of its life. Erected by the students of the W.E. Cormack Academy, Stephenville, Newfoundland.[389]

In Newfoundland, a memorial in Cormack's honour has been erected by the Historic Sites and Monuments Board of Canada on the road to Random Island. It consists of a large boulder with a plaque attached to it:

William Epps Cormack, 1796–1868. Born in St. John's, Cormack was educated at the University of Edinburgh. In 1822, with Joseph Sylvester, A Micmac, he began, from this locality, a journey on foot across the unmapped interior of Newfoundland which he completed in 58 days. He published his data on the flora, fauna, and geology in the Edinburgh Philosophical Journal in 1824 and his complete account, Journey across Newfoundland, in 1856. He founded the Beothuck Institute, and, for a few months before her death, shared his home with Shanawdithit, the last known member of her tribe. He died in British Columbia.[390]

His friend and obituarist, John Robson, stated that "the impulse of a strong fancy made him a wanderer—the commercial man and the explorer in one … He was naturally of a buoyant and happy disposition, genial and kindly; his manners were suave and dignified,"[391] an apt summary of Cormack's life journey and his personality.

Acknowledgements

The author is greatly indebted to Robyn Fleming, who did research, inserted the endnotes, and helped with this publication in many ways. I gratefully acknowledge the permission from the *Newfoundland and Labrador Studies* to use material from my and the late Alan G. Macpherson's two articles: "William Eppes Cormack, A Biographical Account of the Early Years" (vol. 31, no. 1 [Spring 2016]) and "William Eppes Cormack: The Later Years" (vol. 32, no. 1 [Spring 2017]). I appreciate Bernard D. Fardy's permission to use his book *William Epps Cormack, Newfoundland Pioneer* for information on Cormack's time in Australia, New Zealand, San Francisco, and British Columbia, because due to COVID-19, I was unable to access my own research material which I had donated to Memorial University's Archive and Special Collections several years ago. I also used material from Michael Rennie, California, with whom Alan and I exchanged research results. I thank James Williamson for his research.

Appendix 1

On the Natural History and Economical Uses of the Cod, Capelin, Cuttle-Fish, and Seal, as they occur on the Banks of Newfoundland, and the Coasts of that Island and Labrador. Communicated in a Letter to Professor Jameson, by W.E. Cormack, Esq.†*

Of the fishes of the British North American Seas, the most abundant is, at the same time, the most important to man. The cod (*Gadus Morhua*) here holds dominion over all the habitable parts of the ocean,—from the outer edges of the great banks of Newfoundland, which are more than 800 miles from land, and more than 100 fathoms deep, to the verges of every creek and cove of the bounding coasts: it even ascends into the fresh-water.

To support such a mass of living beings, the ocean sends her periodical masses of other living beings; and these, in the economy of nature, are next in importance, and, of necessity, in abundance in these seas. Nature furnishes two successive tribes of animals as food for one tribe; and for the three together, this busiest part of the ocean seems to exist.

---

*   Read before the Wernerian Natural History Society, 14 January 1826.

†   The interesting details in this communication are the result of the author's inquiries and observations in Newfoundland. Mr. Cormack, who is an active and intelligent Newfoundland merchant, has already distinguished himself, by being the first European who succeeded in crossing Newfoundland: of which achievement an account, with a map of the route, was published in the 10th volume of the Edinburgh Philosophical Journal, p. 56. et seq.-Ep.

The Cod.—The cod is accompanied at one season by shoals of myriads of the capelin (*Salmo arcticus*), and at another by equal hosts of that molluscous animal the cuttle-fish (*Sepia Loligo*), called in Newfoundland the Squid. The three animals are migratory; and man, who stations himself on the shores for their combined destruction, conducts his movements according to their migrations. By art, he captures annually more than two hundred millions of the cod with the capelin, and one hundred millions with the cuttle-fish. On the coast of Labrador, and in the north part of Newfoundland, the cod is so abundant, that it is hauled on shore with lines in vast quantities. Thus, by these three means, and the use of herrings and shell-fish for bait, along the southern shores of the Gulf of Saint Lawrence, there is caught in the British North American Seas, upwards of *four hundred millions of cod annually.*

There appear to be four varieties or kinds of the cod in these seas; but their history has not been sufficiently attended to, to determine their relations to each other as species or variety. The first is the bank-cod, found on the great bank, many miles from land; the second is the shore-cod, caught in the bays around the shores, and in the Gulf of Saint Lawrence; the third is the red-cod (*Gadus callarias*), resembling the rock-cod or red-ware codling of Scotland, caught near the shores; the fourth and most remarkable, is what may be called the Seal-headed cod, from its head resembling that of a seal or dog. The haddock (*Gadus Æglefinus*), of a large size, is also met with among the proper cod. All the kinds approach towards one size, and are caught and dried promiscuously by the fishermen. The bank-cod differs from the other varieties in his place of resort, which is almost always on the banks, at a distance from land; he is also larger and stronger, with larger scales and spots; his body is of a lighter colour throughout, with the spots more generally diffused, and more distinctly marked; his flesh, too, is firmer. The shore-cod resembles most the cod in a healthy state on the coasts of Britain, and is that of which the greatest quantity is caught, owing to its being most conveniently taken: the back is of a dusky brown colour; the belly, silvery or yellowish, and the spots in general not remarkably distinct. The red cod is, probably, larger than our rock-cod, and is not numerous. The seal-headed cod, is of the same colour and size as the shore-cod; and its head is, in like manner, covered with skin; and it is comparatively rare. The young cod, tom-cod, or podley, swarms in summer in all the harbours and shallow-waters.

There are some other differences in the cod, which may partly arise from difference of latitude and of coasts where they are found. Thus, the farther north, the less oil is obtained from them, their livers being smaller; and the bank-cod yields the least oil of any. The cod is sometimes caught six feet in length; but there are accounts of its having been taken larger. All the kinds of cod obey the same general laws of migration. They shift according to the changes of temperature in their element, arising from the seasons, and with the supplies of food which invariably accompany these changes. The bank-cod seems to be the most stationary.

As we advance northward from the Gulf of Saint Lawrence, the migrations of the cod assume a more decided character, and it strikes in greater abundance. This holds as far north as fishing-posts have yet been established on the coast of Labrador. The same applies to the migrations and abundance of the other fishes inhabiting these seas, more especially of those connected with the cod, and they arise together from the same general causes. In the Gulf of Saint Lawrence, Lat. 45° 48°, particularly along the shores of Nova Scotia, New Brunswick, Canada, and the adjacent islands, where shell-fish are more abundant than farther to the north, and where, perhaps, in consequence, more other fishes remain during the winter, the herring‡ arrives in spring, about the same time that it arrives on the coasts of Newfoundland and Labrador, in April and May, when the cod, in consequence, becomes probably equally abundant at all places; but afterwards, worlds of food arrive on the coasts of Newfoundland and Labrador; first the capelin over the shores of both these countries, and then, again, the cuttle-fish, around the shores of Newfoundland; they never failing to bring in with them their hosts of cod, and to retain them at these shores during the summer. Neither the capelin, nor any equivalent, ever appears at the countries farther south, although the cuttle-fish visits, and sometimes in considerable quantities, the east coast of Nova Scotia and Cape Breton: *Hence* the pre-eminence of Newfoundland and Labrador as a fishing-station, over every other part of the northern hemisphere.

At Labrador, and in the north part of Newfoundland, where the length of the summer is not more than six weeks or two months, the hook and line are often laid aside for the seine; for it is necessary that enough of cod should be taken within the first two or three weeks, otherwise the remainder of the warm weather would not be sufficient to dry it. Hence the cod-fishery, according to the present mode of curing, which is, with the exception of a very trifling proportion, by drying the fish in the sun, cannot be carried on farther north than a certain latitude.

‡   The Alewife or Gaspereau visits the coasts of the countries just named, Nova Scotia, &c., but is never met with at Newfoundland, nor farther north.

The fishery of Newfoundland commences in June, as soon as the capelin appears on the coast, and ends about the beginning of September, when the cuttle-fish begins to move off from the shores. The capelin is the bait used during the first month or six weeks, and after that the cuttle-fish.

When bait is scarce, considerable numbers of cod are caught by *jigging*: the *jiggers* being an artificial bait, with hooks affixed.

The process of curing the cod requires about a month in favourable weather.

Of the four hundred millions and upwards of cod that are taken annually out of the British North American Seas, about one hundred millions, or upwards of sixty thousand tons, are exported in a dried state by the British, to the warm countries of Europe and America: Of the remainder, a part equal to double that of the British is taken away by the Americans,—a part by the French,—and a part is consumed in the countries themselves.

It is from the livers of the cod-fish, that the cod-oil of commerce is made. These are exposed in casks, and sometimes in **vats**, to the sun, and the heat in all these countries is sufficient to render them into oil[§]. There is a falling off, some years, in the average quantity of oil obtained from the cod throughout the British fisheries; but as the French have the exclusive privilege of fishing at those parts of the island where the different kinds of fish abound most, it is probable that the quantity of oil in proportion to the quantity of fish caught, including all the fisheries, in any one year may not vary much.

As the sun withdraws from the north, the temperature of the

[§]   There ought to be obtained from all the cod caught, twenty-five thousand *tons* of oil, about five to six thousand tons of which are exported by the British, to Britain.

surface-water decreases; its vivifying principle vanishes, and it is no longer inviting to the free inhabitants of the deep. The cuttle-fish begins to retire, and with it man ends his warfare with the cod. All feel the warning, and begin to retire to the strong holds in their respective elements, leaving the field of their industry and summer rejoicing, where air, earth, and water, had met in harmony together, soon to become the conflicting scene of an arctic winter.

Of the Capelin.—The value of this delicate and interesting little fish may be estimated, when it is known to constitute the bait with which more than half the cod caught in these seas are taken. The capelin arrives on the coasts of these countries to spawn about the end of June, and departs about the end of July and beginning of August. It arrives at Labrador about a month later, and remains from two to four months. Its numbers are often truly wonderful. Immediately on its arrival, it pushes its dense shoals into the small bays and creeks, as if to shun the jaws of the millions of its devouring enemies, the cod, and many other fishes which had followed it from the deep, and which remain arrayed at a little distance, impatient for its destruction. These massive clouds of capelin are sometimes more than fifty miles long, and many miles broad. Their spawn is sometimes thrown up along the beaches, forming masses of considerable thickness, most of which is carried back into the sea by a succeeding tide or two.

The capelin is six or seven inches in length; although the males sometimes occur nearly twice the ordinary size. It is caught for bait, in nets constructed of different forms for the purpose. It possesses some peculiar quality, which unfits it to be cured for domestic use like the herring, and is, therefore, merely dried in the sun. Whether the migration of the capelin is to and from the north-sea, or limited to the adjacent deep-waters, does not appear to be yet well ascertained, notwithstanding that its appearance and disappearance at all parts of these coasts are watched, as important events, by every fisherman. On the great scale, it is as regular and certain in its appearance and disappearance, as the herring is on the coasts of Europe. It generally appears some days earlier at the south-east parts of Newfoundland, than at the neighbouring parts of the island farther to the north; and from its leading in the bank-cod to these places (as in 1825), it would seem to have come in from the Great Bank. There is little doubt that it is on the banks at certain seasons, as is shown not merely by the circumstance of its appearing to have led in the cod from thence towards the shores, but by the fact, that, very early in spring, and some weeks before it appears every where at the shores, the cod on the banks take it very readily as a bait salted, when, at the same time, the cod at the shore will not take it in that state. It is well known, that the cod will take readily as a bait, on the great scale, that only which is its common food at the time; and, in the present case, as soon as the capelin arrives at the shores, the bank-cod, which we infer to have followed it from the banks, not only continue to take it salted[¶], but the shore-cod which refused it before, now take it fresh and salted promiscuously**.

The Cuttle-Fish.—About the beginning of August, the throngs of capelin which had enlivened the shores, give way to throngs of the cuttle-fish. This animal seems to succeed the other, as if to supply

---

[¶]   The capelin are salted the preceding year purposely, to fish for the cod on the banks earlier in the ensuing spring than the cod nearer the shore can be caught; that is before the capelin has struck in.

**   The capelin is also sometimes taken in the month of April, by the sealing vessels, among the ice on the banks, more than 200 miles from the land; and then it is found also in the stomachs of the seals;—no doubt on its migration at that time from the deeps over the banks towards the coast.

immediately provision to the cod. It is of equal importance in Newfoundland as the capelin, as it is the bait with which the other half of the cod here is caught

The cuttle-fish does not appear at Labrador in quantities the same as at Newfoundland;—from which it might be inferred that it migrates only to and from the adjacent deep waters.

The common size of this animal is from 6 to 10 inches in length; but it has been met with of colossal size. During violent gales of wind, hundreds of tons of them are often thrown up together in beds on the flat beaches, the decay of which spreads an intolerable effluvium around. It begins to retire from the coast in September. It is made no use of except for bait; and as it maintains itself in deeper water than the capelin, instead of nets being used to take it, it is jigged; a jigger being a number of hooks radiating from a fixed centre, made for the purpose. The cod is in best condition after having fed on it.

When shoals of the cuttle-fish and of the capelin come in contact, the latter always retreat, and from the wounds they carry with them, are sufferers in an attack: These animals dart backwards and forwards with a quickness which the capelin cannot escape.

The cuttle-fish is supposed to impart the crimson colour which the sea exhibits in various parts here, during the latter part of summer. The water of the harbour of St John's, two miles in extent, sometimes exhibits the phenomenon.

It may be unnecessary to say that the migrations of the cod, of the capelin, and of the cuttle-fish, are only once a year[††].

††   The cuttle-fish occurs in abundance in many of our estuaries and coasts, but has hitherto been considered as of no value. Now that it is known to form an excellent bait for cod, and even for other fishing, it is not to be doubted that it will in future, in this country, be used with equal advantage and profit as a bait for the capture of our cod, ling, &c—ED.

Of the Seals.—Newfoundland, owing to its projecting into the Atlantic eastward from Labrador, intercepts many of the immense fields and islands of ice, which, in the spring, move south from the Arctic Sea. These fields of ice, in their original formation, present, at their edges, a sufficient barrier against the inroads of the ocean; and they are so extensive, that their interior parts, with the openings or lakes interspersed, notwithstanding the rage of elements around, remain serene and unbroken: Here are the chosen transitory abodes of millions of seals,—here these animals enjoy months of peace and security, to bring forth and nurture their young. Such fields collect on the coasts of Newfoundland, and, as it were, offer to the inhabitants the treasures they bring: The island is periodically surrounded by them for many leagues in all directions,—the inhabitants within the dazzling bulwark being as impotent towards the rest of the world, as the rest of the world is towards them.

The all-efficient sun, gradually returning, liberates the fields of ice from the shores to which they had for a time become attached, and enables man again to expose himself with impunity in his own element.

In the month of March, upwards of 800 vessels, fitted out for the seal-fishery, are extricated from the icy harbours on the east coast of Newfoundland;—the fields are now all in motion, and the vessels plunge directly into the edges of such as appear to have seals on them;—the crews, armed with heavy firelocks and bludgeons, there *land*, and, in the course of a few weeks, destroy nearly 300,000 of these animals for their fat and skins. The skins, with the fat which surrounds the body, are taken off together, and the scalped carcases left on the ice. When the vessels are loaded with these scalps, or otherwise, when the ice is scattered and dissolved by the advancing spring, which it always is, except the islands, before the middle of

May, they return to their respective ports; the fat is then separated from the skins, and exposed in vats to the heat of the sun, where, in from three to five weeks, it is rendered into the seal oil of commerce[‡‡]. The field-ice extends, with interruptions, more than 200 miles off the land, but the vessels in general have not to go so far to look for the seals: The fields are even met with at sea continuous in a northerly and southerly direction for that extent, at that distance from land.

As these fields of ice are not formed at Newfoundland, and only partially formed at Labrador, the herds of seals which are found on them, when they appear at these places, must have come from the sea farther north, where the main body of the ice is formed, viz. from the Greenland Sea, and that in the vicinity of Davis' Straits. The Greenland winter, it would appear, is too severe for these animals, and when it sets in, they accompany the field-ice, which winds and currents carry south-ward, and remain on it until it is scattered and dissolved in the ensuing spring, in about Lat. 43° N., or about 200 miles south of Newfoundland. Old and young of these animals being then deserted in the ocean by their birth-place, nature points out to them the course to their favourite icy haunts, and thither their herds hurry over the deep to pass an arctic summer. Winter returns, and with it commences again their annual migration from latitude to latitude.

There are five different kinds of seals found on the field-ice at Newfoundland, all known in the Greenland seas. The three best known of which are, 1st, The Harp (*Phoca groenlandica*), the one-year old of which is called the Bedlimmer; 2d, The Hood or Hooded Seal (*Phoca leonina,*); and, 3d, The Square flipper.

[‡‡]   From 3000 to 4000 tons of seal oil, according to the success of the fishery, is made annually. The seal fishery is prosecuted by the British only.

The other two kinds are the Blue Seal, so called from its colour, which is as large as the Hooded Seal; and the Jar Seal, so named from its form resembling that of a jar, thick at the shoulders, and tapering off suddenly towards the tail; head small, body 4 or 5 feet long, the fur spotted, and it keeps more in the water than the other ice-seals. These all differ from the shore or harbour-seal (*Phoca vitulina*) of these coasts. The ice-seals are alike migratory, and promiscuously gregarious; they differ much in size, and the flesh of them all is very unpalatable, unless to an acquired taste, more particularly that of the old ones, differing in this respect from the flesh of the shore-seal, some parts of which are very good. It remains to be proved, that some of the alleged differences in the ice-seals do not arise from age. Although the ice-seals, which are sometimes met with in herds of many leagues in extent on the ice, seem to have no ordinary means of subsistence, yet the hand of unerring Providence maintains both old and young excessively fat. The seal-hunters often find fresh capelin and other animal substances in their stomachs.

Notwithstanding the apparently immense annual destruction by man among the cod in these seas for more than two centuries, it does not appear that their numbers are at all diminished, or that their migrations are in any way affected: Nor is it likely that they ever will be, if we may judge from the migratory fishes of Europe that have been persecuted for many more centuries, between the North Cape and the South of England.

It is not so, however, with those animals which man can pursue in his own element;—thus, the walrus and the penguin, once abundant, may be said now to have entirely disappeared from the Gulf of St Laurence.

As the persecution of the seals in the field-ice increases, which it has, every year since it commenced, it will be interesting to observe, at some future day not far distant, the effect on their numbers. It is not much more than thirty years since any vessels ventured out among the ice at sea, purposely equipped and manned for their destruction.

The cod, the capelin, and the cuttle-fish, in their natural connection, and the seal, or rather the cod and the seal, constitute the political value of Newfoundland and Labrador; and render these otherwise desolate and inhospitable regions the scene of rivalry of British, French, and American national enterprise and industry[§§]. The day is not far distant. when vessels will be fitted out direct from Britain for the seal-fishery at Newfoundland.

[§§] The herring, mackerel, and whale, are in abundance at Newfoundland, and comparatively allowed to pass unmolested. The herring varies in size, from small to several pounds weight. The whale is of three or four kinds, and the fishery of it is prosecuted only by one enterprising English mercantile house at the south part of the island; the whales have been taken upwards of 70 feet in length, yielding from six to eight tons of oil. The salmon abounds in all the rivers, and is taken in large quantities. The dog-fish sometimes occurs with the cod in great numbers.

Appendix 2

Memorandum of the Locality of the Bone of the Dinornis Giganteus *found in the north part of New Zealand in 1849. For Professor Owen.*

"The Bone" of the *Dinornis Giganteus* now presented to Professor Owen was found in the north part of the North Island of New Zealand, in the month of January, 1849. Its locality was in a small bay called Opito, at the east extremity of the projecting land between Mercury Bay and Wangapous on the east coast, in about the latitude of 36°40'S, and fifty miles east from Auckland. The bay is about a mile in length, northerly and southerly, by about half a mile in depth, with high bluff heads or rocky cliffs projecting at each extremity; the semicircular sandy beach inside forming the bay. An irregular strip of low land lies inside of the beach, in some parts fertile, in other parts consisting of downs, and is overlooked in the rear by round hills of from 100 to 300 feet in height. The hills are composed of yellow-white and red burnt earth; very barren, producing stunted fern, and a solitary bush or scrubby tree here and there. Towards the north end of the bay a small brook discharges itself, from a swamp at the foot of the hills in the rear: and at the mouth of the brook a short range of downs runs along the beach to the southward, presenting a line of earthy cliffs, wasting away and forming the shore as they fall down by the washing of the sea at the foot. These cliffs are about from twenty-five to thirty-five feet in height, and nearly perpendicular. The upper stratum of the cliffs is formed of sand and is about three feet in thickness, producing the usual arenaceous shrubs, grasses, etc. Underneath, the line of demarcation being very distinct, is a thick stratum or bed of sandy earth, sand predominating: out of this substratum, about fifty or sixty yards south of the mouth of the brook, the Moa's bones were exposed, projecting, in consequence of a late falling away of that part of the cliff in which they were imbedded: they lay a foot or more beneath the upper surface of the substratum. At the same spot there was a *"kapura maori"* or native cooking fireplace, dug into the surface of the substratum, and full of stones that had been once heated (to convey the heat to the food laid upon them), and left, just as similar cooking-places are left at the present day by the natives;— about two feet from which lay the bones. Close to the fireplace, and similarly imbedded, were bones of smaller birds, and of fishes similar to those found at present in the sea adjacent; all, including those of the Moa, having been evidently the remains of the food cooked here in a former period and eaten, as my native attendant remarked, by the then native inhabitants. A part of a leg bone, about two feet in length, apparently belonging to the same leg as this femur,[¶¶] the bone having been broken near the middle (probably in order to be placed more conveniently over the fireplace), was also found close to the femur.

The antiquity of these remains can only be arrived at by inference. How long it is since the superficial stratum of sand now exhibited at the top of the cliffs overlooking the sea, was formed by water and winds, is a matter of induction from the geologist. The sea is now

¶¶   It accords with the size of the tibea of the *Dinornis gracilis.* RO.

undoing, and claiming the privilege of, former lacustrine or marine deposits. It would not be difficult to compute, with some shadow of approximation, the time required for the inroad of the ocean into strata of the nature of those described, supposing them to have extended from the summit of the cliffs to the ocean half a mile distant, along a line between the two heads or extremities of the bay: but that period would be conjectural only; for there are rocks, inlets, and islands succeeding each other—mile beyond mile,—extending into the surrounding ocean, all of which are, by marine inroad, vestiges only of former rock-formations. Man and the *Moa*, however, were coeval at man's cooking fireplace upon this substratum.

[drawing of profile of strata:]
3 feet thick, surface stratum of sand
underneath: bones   old native fireplace
underneath: substratum of sandy earth,
    30 feet above level of the Sea.

The mother ocean is altering, in some places very rapidly, the configuration of the coast of New Zealand. It is consuming some parts, and forming others by deposits; and again removing former deposits. In a general view, many parts of the east coast of the North Island are being disintegrated, not to reappear above water for many ages; while on the west coast, downs are not only being formed, stretching into the sea, but superimposing themselves—inland—in some places.

These shiftings of the outline of the earth's crust are not limited to the sea-coast: for in the interior are many partial and violent settlings of the earth, evidently from earthquakes; submerging, in some instances many feet under the surface of fresh-water lakes, land with the natives' houses, fences etc. upon it. This has happened in regard to the lake situated some miles from the east bank of the River Waipa, and south-eastwardly from the ruins of the famous sacked Pa (town) called "Matakitaki."

W.E. Cormack

6 Percy Street, 22 October 1850.

To Professor Owen,
Royal College of Surgeons,
London.

Endnotes

1   His middle name has also appeared as "Epps" or "Epes."

2   For three examples, among others: William E. Cormack, "Account of a Journey across the Island of Newfoundland, Esq. In a letter addressed to the Right Hon. Earl Bathurst, Secretary of State for the Colonies, &&—with a Map of Mr. Cormack's Journey across the Island of Newfoundland," *Edinburgh Philosophical Journal* 10, no. 19 (1824): 156–62; "Mr. Cormack's Journey in Search of the Red Indians in Newfoundland. Read before the Boeothick Institution at St. John's, Newfoundland," *Edinburgh New Philosophical Journal* 20, no. 6 (1829): 318–29; *Narrative of a Journey across the Island of Newfoundland, the Only Ever Performed by a European* (St. John's: Morning Post and Commercial Journal, 1856).

3   J.P. Howley, *The Beothucks or Red Indians* (Cambridge: Cambridge University Press, 1915); Ingeborg Marshall, *A History and Ethnography of the Beothuk* (Montreal and Kingston: McGill-Queen's University Press, 1996).

4   The Rooms Public Archives Division (hereafter TRPAD), GN 2/39/A, Census of St. John's for 1794–95. By 1794–95, c.3,250 inhabitants were listed. The figure of about 3,000 for 1782 is an estimate.

5   Many references to an Alexander Cormack, or some variation of that name, were examined in Scottish, New England, and Quebec holdings without success.

6   TRPAD, GN 2/1/A, vol. 13–15, 1797–1800, box 5, Colonial Office Outgoing Correspondence, vol. 13, ff. 369–70, Oct. 16, 1797, Principal Merchants of St. John's to Governor William Waldegrave, regarding the location of a market.

7   TRPAD, GN 2/1/A, vol. 11–12, box 4, 1786–1797; vol. 12, ff. 296–97, Oct. 29, 1794, Cormack listed as member of the Grand Jury.

8   The National Archives of the UK (hereafter TNA, UK), HO 46/76, formerly HO 76/1, Aug. 1793, gives Cormack as owner of the *Nancy*; Public Archives Record Office (hereafter PARO), PEI, Acc. 4063, United Empire Loyalist collection. Reel 1: St. John's Island (PEI), Collector of Customs Letter Book 1784–99, Shipping Inwards entry books (4 vols.) 1790–1822, May 27, 1799, lists Cormack as owner of the *Two Sisters*; K. Matthews, Memorial University of Newfoundland (hereafter Memorial University), Maritime History Archives (hereafter MHA), Name File "Alexander Cormack," GN 5/2/A/1, box 24, Supreme Court Records (1798–1802), f. 37, Dec. 11, 1798, Cormack was sued, as his brig *Rose* had struck William Pendergast's wharf; TNA, UK, BT 6/190, Returns of Shipping, Quebec, 1787–94, shows W.I. Eppes and A. Cormack as owners of the *Betsey*. These references also describe ships' cargoes and ports of call.

9   TRPAD, CO 194/39, 1780–84, ff. 276–77, Dec. 16, 1784, Petition to Lieutenant Governor Ilford with the signature of "Robert McAuslan." His name has also been spelled McAusland, McAuslin, McAuslane, or Mcaslan.

10   TRPAD, GN 2/39/A, Census of St. John's, 1794–95, "Robert McAuslan, 19 years in the country, married, 1 male, 1 female, both Protestants"; *Mormon's International Genealogical Index (MIG)*, Janet Mcaslan born Mar. 1774 in Glasgow to Robert Mcaslan (merchant) and Grizzel (Wright); an older brother, Peter, was born in 1772, and a younger sister (not named) was born Oct. 15, 1776. The sister is not listed in the 1794–95 census of St. John's.

11   TRPAD, GN 2/1/A, vol. 11–12, 1786–97, box 4, vol. 11, Colonial Secretary's Office, Outgoing Correspondence, p. 419, Oct. 17, 1778, Governor John Elliot to Joseph Peers, recommending Robert McAuslan as Deputy Postmaster.

12   TRPAD, GN 2/39/A, Census of St. John's, 1794–95, entry #262.

13   TRPAD, Cathedral of St. John the Baptist Church of England burials, 1796–1803, box 1, Aug. 14, 1796, Alexander Cormack.

14   Benjamin Lester Diaries (1761–1802), Dec. 27, 1783, Lester writes that his good friend, British MP Joseph Gulson, "got [Eppes] made a purser. Wrote Mr. Eppes to acquaint him of it." MHA, Garland–Lester Family Fonds on microfilm. Digital Archives Initiative (hereafter DAI), Memorial University Libraries, http://collections.mun.ca.

15   TRPAD, GN 2/1/A, vol. 13–15, box 5, 1797–1800, Colonial Secretary's Office, Outgoing Correspondence, vol. 14, f. 182, Mar. 10, 1798, Instructions to William Isham Eppes Esq., Commissary of Stores and Provisions at Newfoundland.

16   Benjamin Lester Diaries (1761–1802), July 6 1792: "Mr. and Mrs. Eppes and Mr. Rouths Son went with Capt. J. Andrews to St. John's." From MHA, Garland-Lester Family Fonds, on microfilm. DAI, Memorial University Libraries, http://collections.mun.ca; http://www.ancestry.ca/genealogy/records/william-isham-eppes_12895842.

17   TRPAD, GN 2/1/A, vol. 13–15, 1797–1800, box 5, Colonial Secretary's Office, Outgoing Correspondence, vol. 13, pp. 333–34, Oct. 13, 1797, Waldegrave to Cormack granting land at River Head.

18   TRPAD, GN 169, vol. 4, Miscellaneous Deeds and Wills, ff. 180–82, Feb. 8, 1808. David Rennie purchased land from Robert Bulley's estate in Outer Cove that included Fir Hill Farm, which had "formerly been leased by Alexander Cormack."

19   Robert MacKinnon, "Farming the Rock: The Evolution of Commercial Agriculture in Newfoundland to 1945," *Acadiensis* 20, no. 2 (1991): 36–38.

20   TRPAD, GN 2/1/A, vol. 13–15, box 5, 1797–1800, Colonial Secretary's Office Outgoing Correspondence; vol. 13, f. 35, Aug. 9, 1797, Governor Waldegrave to Magistrates of St. John's, recommendation for a market; vol. 13, ff. 369–70, Oct. 16, 1797, merchants to Waldegrave describing the site for the market and the intent to construct a slaughterhouse.

21   C.G. Head, *Eighteenth Century Newfoundland* (Toronto: McClelland and Stewart, 1976), 209–14.

22   TRPAD, CO 194/39, 1796–97, f. 286, Dec. 17, 1797, Waldegrave sent Eppes's report on the spoiled provisions to the Duke of Portland, Colonial Secretary; f. 288, Eppes to Waldegrave, sent from Poole, Dec. 13, 1797, warning of impending food scarcity.

23   TRPAD, GN 2/1/A, vol. 13–15, 1797–1800, vol. 14, ff. 392–93, Oct. 15, 1798, Waldegrave to Eppes, granting permission for Eppes to go to England, providing he return with the spring convoy.

24   Eppes to Lord Commissioners of His Majesty's Treasury, transmitting vouchers of purchases of provision made by Cormack, acting Commissary of Provisions. Great Britain, D'Alberti Papers (correspondence, incoming and outgoing, between the Colonial Office and the Governor's Office in Newfoundland), vol. 9, May 20, 1795, p. 270. London, Colonial Office, paper held in the Centre for Newfoundland Studies (hereafter CNS), DAI, Memorial University Libraries, http://collections.mun.ca/PDFs/cns_colonia/A51_V09.pdf.

25   P. O'Neill, *The Oldest City: The Story of St. John's, Newfoundland* (Portugal Cove-St. Philip's: Boulder Publications, 2003), 65. To make matters worse, a fire broke out at Fort William in March, destroying medical supplies, bedding, utensils, and food stores.

26   Eppes to Lord Commissioners, submitting vouchers for provisions made by Cormack "for the use of His Majesty's Troops" that was "in conformity to an order by Colonel Thomas Skinner, Commandant." Great Britain, D'Alberti Papers, vol. 9, May 20, 1798, London, Colonial Office. Paper text held in CNS, http://collections.mun.ca/PDFs/cns_colonia/A51_V09.pdf. In January 1799, there was another substantial loss of food at the garrison due to improper shipment and storage, and Waldegrave called for Eppes's dismissal. Yet, Eppes continued to serve as Commissary for another four years, though he had to resign from his position as an officer in the Fencibles. TRPAD, GN 2/1/A, vol. 13–15, 1797–1800, vol. 15, ff. 137–38, Jan. 22, 1799, Waldegrave to the Duke of Portland; TRPAD, CO 194/43, f. 41, Apr. 20, 1802, J. Gambier to Lord Hobart, refers to W.I. Eppes as Commissary in Newfoundland. *The London Gazette*, July 13, 1799, announced Eppes's resignation from the Fencibles.

27   Waldegrave to the Charitable Fund Committee, Great Britain, D'Alberti Papers, vol. 9, p. 190, Oct. 23, 1798; Church of England Fundraising Committee to Governor Waldegrave, vol. 7, p. 310, Oct. 24, 1797.

28   TRPAD, GN 169, Miscellaneous Deeds & Wills, Index 1744–1869, vol. 2, 1798–1804, p. 117, "Memorandum of the original Bill of Sale from the assigns of R.H. Roope." The property was located near "Upper Pie Corner," or "Brookes's Plantation." Originally half the property was sold to Marmaduke Hart, W.I. Eppes, and Alexander Cormack, but on November 20, 1799, Hart and Eppes sold their share to Cormack, so that he owned a moiety; the other half was owned by George Elliot.

29   PARO, Land Registry Records, Conveyances, Liber 8(2) ff. 66–67, Aug. 24, 1795. Peter McAuslan bought the land from Thomas Rhodes Haszard of Charlottetown.

30   PARO, RG 8, vol. 770–72, June 13, 1803, "to Robert McAusland from Edmund Fanning, Town Lot #98 in the 4th hundred" and "Robert McAusland of Ch'tn, gentleman, granted from L. Gov. also Lot #549." The land was granted by the colonial governor, Edmund Fanning, for no money.

31   TRPAD, GN 5/2/A/1, Supreme Court Central, Minutes, box 24, 1798–1803 and 1802–1805, f. 117, Dec. 15, 1800, Alexander Cormack vs. John Rennels; Dec. 18, 1800, Alex Cormack, treasurer of the School Committee vs. Peter McKie.

32   There is no birth record for Janet Grace Cormack, but her death, under her married surname "Scott," is recorded in the MIC Return 1861 for Kensal Manor House, Willesden, UK. Registration District of Hendon 135/3, f. 135; RG 9/785:3 (Willesden): "Janette Grace [Scott] age 61, [born] Nfld. 1799/1800."

33   Dr. Alan G. Macpherson, personal communication with author: Grizel derives from the older Scots Gaelic name "Greasesail."

34 Keith Matthews, "Newfoundland Merchants" (1980), Part 1, unpublished manuscript, Memorial University, MHA, entry on John Cunningham.

35 National Records of Scotland (hereafter NRS), RD 5/268, pp. 518–31, Marriage contract and last Will and Testament made on May 22, 1824, between Janette Grace Cormack and William Scott. The document only refers to two siblings, William Eppes and John Bell, with whom she shared property in Newfoundland. The older daughter is not referred to after the census of 1796–97 and could have died any time before that date.

36 TRPAD, Cathedral of St. John the Baptist, Church of England burials, 1796–1803, box 1.

37 TRPAD, GN 5/2/A/9, Supreme Court Central Estate Matters, box 101, Administrations and Probates, 1803–07, pp. 17–22, Aug. 15, 1803.

38 TRPAD, GN 5/2/A/9, Supreme Court Central Estate Matters, box 101, Administrations and Probates, 1803–07, contain a number of wills signed with an *x* or another mark, ff. 29, 38, 42.

39 Trudi Jane Johnson, "Matrimonial Property Law in Newfoundland to the End of the 19th Century" (PhD diss., Memorial University, 1998), 48.

40 TRPAD, GN 5/2/A/9, Supreme Court Administrations and Probates, box 101, 1803–07, ff. 17–22, Aug. 15, 1803.

41 TRPAD, GN 5/2/A/9, Supreme Court Administrations and Probates, box 101, 1803–07, ff. 17–22, Aug. 15, 1803.

42 TRPAD, GN 2/1/A, vol. 12, f. 296, Oct. 29, 1794, Chief Justice D'Ewes Coke to Governor Wallace. David Rennie, Richard Reed, and Alexander Cormack with 20 others were on the Grand Jury for the trial concerning the murder of Lieutenant Lawry.

43 Gordon Handcock, *So longe as there comes noe women: English Migration and Settlement* (St. John's: Breakwater, 1989), 279. The value of several wealthy fish merchants' estates at their death, listed in 1793, was between £20,000 and £130,000.

44 TRPAD, GN 169, vol. 9, Miscellaneous Deeds and Wills (1815–16), sale of Elliot's moiety of Roope's Plantation to Janet Cormack, 1804. Although this document was created in 1804, it was included in vol. 9.

45 TRPAD, GN 5/1/A/4, Supreme Court, Central Circuit, Writs, box 3, 1800–07, f. 42, granted on Dec. 3, 1804.

46 TRPAD, GN 169, vol. 3, Miscellaneous Deeds and Wills, 1744–1858, p. 40, Dec. 31, 1804.

47 TRPAD, MG 907, Eastaff, Plan of St. John's, 1807.

48 Public Archives and Record Office of PEI (hereafter PARO PEI), Acc 4063, United Empire Loyalist collection, Reel 1: St. John's island (PEI), Collector of Customs Letter Book, Shipping Inwards entry books (4 vols.) 1790–1822, Dec. 16, 1805.

49 J.F. O'Mara, "Rennie's Mill," *Newfoundland Quarterly* 92, no. 2 (1998): 17.

50 MHA, Matthews Name File, "Stewart": David Rennie was St. John's agent for the firm, 1790–1804 and 1807–10.

51 Glasgow Old Parish Register (OPR) 644.1/52, Jan. 7, 1823: David Rennie died of a "bloodburst," age 58.

52 Scottish Record Society, Roll of Edinburgh Burgesses and Guild Brethren, 1761–1841, "8 Dec. 1791, John Wright … apprentice to James Carfrae."

53   NRS, St. Cuthbert's Parish's "blotter" register MR 4-52, Apr. 23, 1806: "that she has resided upwards of six weeks in Edinburgh is certified by Mr. John Wright, merchant, Edinburgh."

54   "Relict" is an archaic form of the term "widow"; NRS, St. Cuthbert Parish "blotter" register, MR 4-52, Apr. 23, 1806.

55   Matthews, "Newfoundland Merchants," Part 2, unpublished typescript: "Stewart" under "Stewarts and Rennie/Resident Agents and Partners in Newfoundland," Memorial University, MHA.

56   TRPAD, GN 169, vol. 2, Miscellaneous Deeds and Wills, pp. 90–91, Oct. 10, 1801: David Rennie bought a house from Geo. Burton "adjoining the house of Mr. Burton's mother."

57   Statutes of Newfoundland 1875–78, Acts of the General Assembly, 1876, p. 14: $180 authorized for road repairs "from Castle Rennie to Playhouse Hill," DAI, http:// collections.mun.ca/cdm/ref/collection/cns/id/152766; Katherine Bellamy, *Weavers of Tapestry* (St. John's: Flanker, 2006), 430.

58   TRPAD, CO 194/45, ff. 119–20, Oct. 20, 1806, David Rennie to Governor Erasmus Gower.

59   There are no Church of England birth records for this period in St. John's, but both David Jr. and James Gower are listed in later family records.

60   Matthews, "Newfoundland Merchants," Part 2; MHA: "James MacBraire."

61   A.H. Clark, *Three Centuries and the Island* (Toronto: University of Toronto Press, 1959), 44 (map), 265. Rennie purchased Lot 23 in 1810 from William Winter.

62   S. Holland, "Prince Edward Island, 1765," reprinted in *Prince Edward Island Magazine* 3, no. 4 (June 4, 1901): 121–26, https://www.canadiana.ca/view/oocihm.8_06876_28/1.

63   NRS, Glasgow (Lanark), OPR 644, vol. 20, f. 515, "David Rennie Mercht & Janet McAslan, a L[awful] daur. Janet Emma, baptized September 14, 1810, Wit[nesse]s Hay Wright & William Stewart."

64   NRS, Glasgow (Lanark), OPR 644, vol. 21, f. 33, "David Rennie Mercht & Janet McAslan a L[awful] son William Frederick, baptized 14 Feb. 1812. Wit[nesse]s William Mills & William Cormack."

65   NRS, Glasgow (Lanark), OPR 644, vol. 22, f. 4, "David Rennie Mercht & Jane McAsland in Tradeston, son Robert Rennie, born 26 April 1814, baptized [date illegible]." Tradeston was part of Glasgow.

66   Glasgow University Archives, Class Catalogues (Catalogus togatorum in Academia Glasguensi), 1794–1838 [R9/1/1]. Innes Addison, *The Matriculate Albums of the University of Glasgow from 1728–1858* (Glasgow: J. MacLehose & Sons, 1913), lists: "8281 1811 Guliemus Cormack f.n. max (1st son of) Alexandri Mercatoris, Newfoundland, brother of 8685 (f.n.) for the Greek class, which was the second year." Also 1813–14 in Classe Logica, (282) Guliemus Cormack and in the same class, under (284) Campbell, Dom. De Glenorchy.

67   Alexander Grant, *The Story of the University of Edinburgh during Its First Three Hundred Years*, 2 vols. (London: Longmans, Green and Co. 1884), 2:433.

68   Addison, *Matriculate Albums*, lists: "8685 1812 Cormack Joannes f. 2dus Alex Quondam Merc. Glas. (onetime Merchant in Glasgow) otherwise John Bell Cormack W.S. 1827 (W.S. writer to the Signet, a lawyer) died in 1870, brother of 8281 entered for a humanity class which was a first year class." Neither of the brothers graduated at Glasgow. Innes

Addison, *The Role of Graduates of the University of Glasgow* (Glasgow: J. MacLehose & Sons, 1898), lists neither of the Cormack sons. However, extremely few students in the arts did graduate, and they often used the class-certificates of their professors as their university certificates; Addison, *Matriculate Albums*. "David Rennie 10834 [1821] fil. N. max. Davidis Merc. Newfoundland." "Frederick Rennie 12260 [1828] filius natu 4tus Davidis Mercatoris in com. de Lanark." "Robert Rennie 12309 [1828] filius natu quintus Davidis Mercatoris in com. de Lanark"; Edinburgh University, Matriculation Roll: Arts, Law, Divinity iii: 1811–29.

69   *Prince Edward Island Gazette*, June 9, 1819: the *Alexander* cleared for Greenock on July 7, 1819, with a cargo of timber. See also PARO RG 9, Collector of Customs, Shipping outward, July 7, 1819; *Prince Edward Island Gazette*, May 22, June 26, 1820, in section entitled "Custom-house."

70   PARO, Land Registry Records, Liber 26, Folio 1, PoA from David Rennie to William Eppes Cormack, dated Apr. 6, 1819, registered July 30, 1819.

71   Orlo Jones and Douglas Fraser, "Those Elusive Immigrants," *The Island Magazine*, no. 16 (1984): 36–41; *Prince Edward Island Gazette*, Sept. 3, 1819, in section entitled "Custom-house."

72   John MacGregor, *Observations on Emigration to British America* (London: Longmans, Rees, Orme, Brown and Green, 1829), 61: note G, letter from W.E. Cormack to John MacGregor, Feb. 14, 1829.

73   *The Daily Patriot* (Charlottetown), Feb. 14, 1906, 8: son John was a particularly skilled sailor and travelled from California to Manila and Hong Kong.

74   PARO RD 6.1 Series 14, July 9, 1819.

75   *Prince Edward Island Gazette*, "Colonial Secretary's Office, February 14th, 1820," Feb. 29, 1820.

76   *Prince Edward Island Gazette*, "Colonial Secretary's Office, Charlotte-Town, October 25th 1820," Nov. 25, 1820, and Jan. 20, 1821.

77   PARO ACC3035/2, Militia general orders issued by Adjutant General Office, Charlotte Town, Jan. 20, 1820.

78   Charles Dickieson, "New Glasgow as It Was 100 Years Ago," *The Island Register* (1920), http://www.islandregister.com/newglasgow.html; John W. Chalmers, *Laird of the West* (Calgary: Detselig, 1981), 3–4.

79   PARO, RG 6, Supreme Court Case Papers, 1820 W.E.C. against D. & J. Kennedy, and 1821 against A. McGregor.

80   PARO, RG 16, Land Conveyances, Liber 28, ff. 74–76, Feb. 24, 1820; ff. 76–78, June 15, 1820.

81   PARO, RG 16, Land Conveyances, Liber 28, ff. 341–45, lots 200, 241, 250, 256, 266, 277, Nov. 10, 1821, registered May 8, 1822.

82   *Prince Edward Island Register* (Charlottetown), Sept. 15, 1829, vol. 6.

83   High Church Glasgow, burial register, OPR 644/52 15/05/1821, p. 195, "Janet S. McAslan, aka Rennie buried 15 May 1821, age 46, wife of D. Rennie, cause of death: anemia."

84   The disposition is referred to in a contract between Janette Grace Cormack and William Scott and was registered at the same time as their marriage contract, May 24, 1824. NRS, RD 5/268, 517–31 (14.a3). The document was written and signed by John Bell Cormack, at the time apprentice to James Arnott W.S.

85   TRPAD, MG 93, William Noad Collection, William R. Noad's *Plan of St. John's*. The original plan is dated 1849; the printed version used by the author has no date. *The Numerical Index to Accompany the Plan of St. John's* used here is listed as 1853, London.

86   TRPAD, MG 93, Noad Collection, *Plan of St. John's*. By 1853, all land that was part of Roope's Plantation had been divided into parcels for dwellings, shops, and other conveniences.

87   Granted to Alexander Cormack in 1797, TRPAD, GN 2/1/A, vol. 13–15, box 5, 1797–1800, Sept. 14, 1797, Cormack to Waldegrave. On June 19, 1848, John Bell Cormack sold his share of this land to Kenneth McLea, Sr.: Newfoundland and Labrador Registry of Deeds, Central District, 11/255.

88   TRPAD, GN 169, vol. 3, Miscellaneous Deeds and Wills, 1744–1858, p. 40, Dec. 31, 1804. This property was probably the one marked on surveyor Thomas Eastaff's 1807 *Map of the Town and Harbour of St. John's in Newfoundland*; TNA, UK, CO 700/Newfoundland and Labrador, 11A 226664, as "43 Mrs. Cormack's ditto [meadow ground] 1 1/2" [acres/roods/perches]" with a house upon it on Signal Hill Road." This reference was provided by archaeologist Gerald Penney.

89   TRPAD, Crown Land Registry, reel 1, Land Grants, B-6-4, Index and Register, 1803–1923, Oct. 20, 1805.

90   This land, which is outside the boundaries of Noad's map, is referred to as owned by Alexander Cormack in a correspondence in the Duckworth Papers, TRPAD, MG 204, reel 3, Series C. General Series, 1811, pp. 1941–42, including a map. It is not mentioned in the probate records, TRPAD, GN 5/2/A/9, Supreme Court Administrations and Probates, box 6 101, 1803–1807, ff. 17–22, Aug. 15, 1803.

91   Howley, *Beothucks*, 130.

92   Cormack, *Narrative*, 1.

93   Howley, *Beothucks*, 130.

94   Cormack, *Narrative*, 5–6.

95   TNA, UK, CO 194/50, ff. 153–88, Capt. David Buchan's report, 1811; Howley, *Beothucks*, 88.

96   *Dictionary of Canadian Biography* (DCB), s.v. "David Buchan," http://www.bioraphi.ca/en/bio/buchan_david_7E.html.

97   TNA, UK, CO 194/50, ff. 183–85, Capt. David Buchan's report of his expedition to Red Indian Lake, 1811; paraphrased in John Barrow, *Chronological History of Voyages into the Arctic Regions* (London: Murray, 1818), App. I, 23.

98   TNA, UK, CO 194/50, ff. 183–85, Capt. David Buchan's report of his expedition to Red Indian Lake, 1811; paraphrased in Barrow, *Chronological History*, App. I, 8–9.

99   Cormack to John Barrow Esquire, Under Secretary to the Admiralty, Edinburgh, July 22, 1823, TNA, UK, CO 194/66, f. 313.

100   Cormack, *Narrative*, 39, and App. [obituary]; *Edinburgh New Philosophical Journal* 20, no. 6 (1829): Professor Robert Jameson (1774–1854) was appointed Regius Professor of Natural History at Edinburgh and Keeper of the University Museum in 1804; he founded the *Edinburgh Philosophical Journal* in 1819; and he was fellow of a large number of British and international societies.

101   Cormack, "Account of a Journey," 158n.

102   Cormack, *Narrative*, 5, 65.

103   *DCB*, s.v. "Sylvester Joe," http://www.biographi.ca/en/bio/joe_sylvester_6E.html; *Encyclopedia of Newfoundland and Labrador* (ENL), s.v. "Sylvester Joe."

104   Throughout his report of the crossing, Cormack refers to him as Joseph or Joe Sylvester or as my Indian, indicating his position as his guide. In a letter from J.S. Christopher to W.E. Cormack, Nov. 10, 1824, Harbour Breton, Christopher refers to him as Joe Silvestre, Cormack Papers, housed in Howley Family Collection, MUN Library Archives and Special Collections, COLL-262, https://collections.mun.ca/digital/collection/archives/id/10593/rec/90; see also Cormack to John Peyton Jr., Oct. 5, 1827, TRPAD, Rowe Coll., MG 134.

105   Cormack, *Narrative*, 5.

106   Howley, *Beothucks*, 130.

107   ENL, s.v. "Charles Fox Bennett"; Howley, *Beothucks*, 130, n.3.

108   W.E. Cormack to Mr. Munby [Mumbee], Aug. 29, 1822, Cormack Papers, https://collections.mun.ca/digital/collection/archives/id/10714/rec/62.

109   CO 194/65, ff. 136–55, CO 194/72, f. 99.

110   Howley, *Beothucks*, 131–68.

111   *The Examiner* (PEI), "Hunters Grave," Jan. 15, 1879, No. 491/2; the story was found by Bridget Cash (Mrs. James O'Connor, 1861–1945), Clifton, PEI, and republished in *The Guardian* of Charlottetown, Feb. 11, 1939, by James Pendergast, a correspondent.

112   Alan Rayburn, *Geographical Names of Prince Edward Island* (Ottawa: Surveys and Mapping Branch of Department of Energy, Mines, and Resources, 1973). The 1879 newspaper account was in turn plagiarized by John Mackinnon in *A Sketch Book, Comprising Historical Incidents, Traditional Tales, and Translations* (Saint John, NB: Barnes and Co. Ltd, 1915), in which the main actors had different names.

113   *Steel's New and Correct Chart of the Island of Newfoundland with Particular Plans of its Harbours on a Large Scale. With an Estimated Scale of 1:675,000, Compiled from Recent Authorities* (London: Steel & Goddard, Chart Sellers to the Admiralty, March 21, 1817).

114   PANL, Baptismal record book, King's Cove, Bonavista Bay: baptismal record Aug. 1, 1829, King's Cove. Cormack Papers also contain a note to Peter Sylvester; presumably Sylvester had told Cormack about him.

115   Howley, *Beothucks*, 168.

116   Cormack, *Narrative*, 95.

117   *DCB*, s.v. "Herron (Hearn) William."

118   R.T. White, "Priest also Walked across Island," *Western Star*, Nov. 30, 1972; Thomas Sears, *Report of the Missions* (Western Newfoundland: Prefecture Apostolic, 1877), 1; Michael Brosnan, *Pioneer History of St. George's Diocese, Newfoundland* (Toronto: Mission Press, 1948), 6.

119   The baptisms were performed between May 30 and June 7, 1820: Archives of the Roman Catholic Archdiocese, St. John's, Index to Baptisms 1820–1836.

120   *Evening Telegram*, Oct. 15, 1973.

121   Edward Wix, *Six Months of a Newfoundland Missionary's Journal, from February to August 1835* (London: Smith, Elder and Company, 1836).

122   "The Following Account of a Journey," *The Public Ledger*, St. John's, Mar. 26, 1844.

123   N. O'Brig, "In Terre Neuve," *L'illustration* 33 (1859): 218.

124   Don Morris, "Wolves, Snow Slides Met on 600 Mile Woods Trek in 1875," *The Express*, Mar. 11, 1992, 26–27.

125   NRS, Old Parish Register (OPR), Deaths 644/01 0520 0429, Glasgow, "13 January 1823, David Rennie, bloodburst, (age) 58"; NRS, SC 36/48/18, ff. 90–93, Inventory of David Rennie's Estate. Mitchell Library, Record of High Church, New Burying Ground, Register of Lairs, No.1, No. 38 (presumed to mean 1st lair [layer?] on gravesite 38), David Rennie, Dripping Isle.

126   Scottish Record Offce, SC 36/65/25, ff. 105r–113v, 118r & 119v, Rennie's 30-page will, read Glasgow, June 6, 1823; NRS, SC 36/48/18, ff. 90–93, Inventory.

127   *A History of the Society of Writers to Her Majesty's Signet with a List of Members from 1594–1890 and Abstract of Minutes, Edinburgh* (Edinburgh: Edinburgh University Press, 1890); *History of the Society of the Writers to His Majesty's Signet* (Edinburgh: Edinburgh University Press, 1936); Glasgow University Archives, Class Catalogues 1794–1838 [R9/1/1].

128   Scottish Record Office, Edinburgh, Old Parish Register, St. Cuthbert's Parish Register, 685.2/40.

129   Scottish Record Office, RD 5/268, pp. 509–31. Both William Eppes and John Bell Cormack were named as trustees, as were three of William Scott's brothers.

130   Scottish Record Office, 1861 Census Return for Kensal Manor House, Willesden [Hendon 135:3, f. 135; RG 9/785:3—Willesden Parish, Middle-sex], William Scott, son, 34, born in Naples (1826–27); Scottish Record Office, Census for 1871 [RG 10/1327:17], Alexander, son, 43, born in Naples (1827–28); Scottish Record Office, 1891, Census for 5 Lower Prospect Place, Southampton, George Scott, unm. [unmarried] 61 (1829–30), General Practitioner, born Naples, Italy.

131   Natural History Museum, Department of Library and Information Services, London, Owen Collection, W.E. Cormack to Professor Owen, Oct. 25, 1850.

132   Cormack, "Account of a Journey," 158n.

133   W.E. Cormack to the Right Honorable Earl Bathurst, Secretary of State for the Colonies, July 22, 1823, TNA, UK, CO 194/66, f. 315; W.E. Cormack to John Barrow Esquire, Under Secretary to the Admiralty, July 22, 1823, TNA, UK, CO 194/66, f. 313; Dr. Barrow to Prof. Jameson, Sept. 18, (1823?); Howley, *Beothucks*, 204; Lord Bathurst to Dr. Barrow, n.d.

134   Cormack, "Account of a Journey," 156–62. A French translation of the paper also exists: "Note sur l'Histoire naturelle de Terre Neuve, extrait d'une lettre de M. Cormack," *Annales des Sciences Naturelles* (1824): 433–36.

135   *Steel's New and Correct Chart*, 1817, was rescued from destruction by W.A. Munn when the Commission of Government dismantled the first provincial museum. In 1953, Mrs. W.A. Munn donated it to Memorial University Libraries.

136   Cormack, "Account of a Journey," 159.

137 J.B. Jukes, *Map of the Island of Newfoundland* (London: J. & C. Walker, c.1842); Richard H. Bonnycastle, *Newfoundland in 1842, Considered in Its Geological and Statistical Relations* (London: Henry Colbourne, 1842); William Kirwin, G.M. Story, and Patrick A. O'Flaherty, eds., *The Reminiscences of James P. Howley: Selected Years* (St. John's: Breakwater Books, 1997).

138 "Remembering Cormack," *Evening Telegram*, Apr. 15, 1972, at the celebration of the 150th anniversary of Cormack's walk across the island in 1822.

139 MHA, name file "W.E. Cormack," Register of Lloyd Underwriter 1818 and 1821.

140 PARO, PEI, Acc. 4063, United Empire Loyalist Collection, RG 9, reel 1, Collector of Customs Shipping Inward, "Aug. 1821, Oak, 42 to, Crew of 2, Capt. Thomas Spratt, owned by W.E. Cormack and others"; "arr. 26 Sept. 1826, Oak, owned by Thomas Spratt."

141 *The Royal Gazette* (Jan. 12, 1828) and *The Public Ledger* (Jan. 22, 1828) announced that the co-partnership business under the firm of Wm. E. Cormack & Co. was dissolved.

142 *Newfoundland Mercantile Journal*, Dec. 29, 1825, 3, advertised in successive issues until Apr. 27, 1826.

143 *Newfoundland Mercantile Journal*, June 15, 1826, 3, advertised in successive issues until July 27, 1826.

144 *Newfoundland Mercantile Journal*, Nov. 3, 1825, 3, advertised in successive issues until Dec. 1, 1825.

145 Cormack's address as listed in the *Post Office Directory of Edinburgh* for the years 1824–25 was 7 Broughton Place, Edinburgh.

146 Class List of the University of Edinburgh, University Library, Ms. Division, 1825: Extracts from Matriculation Roll: Arts, Law, Divinity, 963: W.E. Cormack, Newfoundland, 5 Lit (course), General and Medical, vol. 21, 1825–26, Matric. No. 1721 Cormack, W.E., Chem.

147 Grant, *Story of the University*.

148 W.E. Cormack, May 20, 1828, to John Stark, Cormack Papers, housed in Howley Family Papers, MUN Library Archives and Special Collections, COLL-262. https://collections. mun.ca/digital/collection/archives/id/10567/rec/76; *Newfoundland Maritime Journal*, no. 636, June 29, 1826: Custom House, St. John's, under "entered": June 24, Schooner *Belinda*, Pitts, Liverpool: "550 hogshead salt, 36 firkins butter, 4 tons coal &c."

149 Edinburgh *New Philosophical Journal* (Apr.–Oct. 1826): 32–41. A summary of this paper was published in ISIS, *Oken's Encyclopaedische Zeitung* (Jena, 1832), 677–79. It was also serialized in the *Daily British Colonist* (Victoria, BC), July 20, 22, 25, 27, 29, 1859, with a new introduction by Cormack.

150 W.E. Cormack to the Hon. & Right Revd. Bishop of Nova Scotia, St. John's, Newfoundland, Jan. 10, 1829, Cormack Papers, https://collections.mun.ca/digital/collection/archives/ id/10702/rec/1; Howley, *Beothucks*, 210; John Nova Scotia, Halifax, Nov. 13 to W.E. Cormack, Esq., Howley, *Beothucks*, 209; John Nova Scotia, River St. Lawrence, Sept. 18, 1828, to W.E. Cormack, Esq., Howley, *Beothucks*, 208.

151 Cormack Papers; *The Royal Gazette*, Nov. 13, 1827; Howley, *Beothucks*, 183–84.

152 Cormack Papers, "Indians" referred to the Abenaki, Innu (Montagnais), and Mi'kmawqguides.

153 Cormack Papers.

154   Cormack Papers.

155   Cormack Papers; *The Royal Gazette*, Nov. 13, 1827.

156   *The Newfoundlander*, Sept. 19, 1827; Cormack travelled on the brig *Dewsbury*.

157   Details about the proceedings of the meeting are quoted from *The Royal Gazette* of Nov. 13, 1827; Howley, *Beothucks*, 182–86.

158   A draft of Cormack's address to the second meeting of the Boeothick Institution included the sentence: "The original idea of founding such an institution emanated from our worthy Vice Patron when at Twillingate in Sept. last," Cormack Papers. This sentence was not included in Cormack's address as recorded by *The Royal Gazette*, Nov. 13, 1827.

159   Inglis (1777–1850) was born in New York, educated in Nova Scotia, and made bishop of Nova Scotia in 1825 with jurisdiction over Newfoundland until 1839; *ENL*, s.v. "John Inglis."

160   John Dunscombe (1778–1847), merchant, was a native of Bermuda. He moved to St. John's in or before 1799 and was involved in the West Indies shipping trade. He was a member of many committees in public service, was appointed aide-de-camp to Governor Cochrane in October 1825 and as such was given the rank of Lieut. Colonel of the Militia, *Dictionary of Newfoundland and Labrador Biography*, s.v. "John Dunscombe."

161   John Stark (1790–1863) was clerk and Registrar of Deeds of the Northern Circuit Court in Harbour Grace, and Prosecutor of the Crown: John P. Greene, *Between Damnation and Starvation: Priests and Merchants in Newfoundland Politics, 1745–1855* (Montreal and Kingston: McGill-Queen's University Press, 1999).

162   Other corresponding members were: from St. John's: Charles Simms; from Harbour Grace: Benjamin Scott; from Fogo: Thomas and David Slade; from Twillingate: The Rev. John Chapman, Robert Tremlett, James Slade, Joseph Simms, Andrew Pearce, Thomas Lyte; from King's Cove: The Rev. Mr. Sinnott; from Britain: "Capt. Hugh Clapperton, R.N. traveler in Africa" who had already died on his second expedition through Central Africa.

163   W.E. Cormack to John Stark, St. John's, May 20, 1828, Cormack Papers, https://collections.mun.ca/digital/collection/archives/id/10567/rec/76.

164   The bishop of Nova Scotia to W.E. Cormack, Halifax, Dec. 21, 1827, Cormack Papers, https://collections.mun.ca/digital/collection/archives/id/10275/rec/68; Howley, *The Beothucks*, 207.

165   W.E. Cormack to the bishop of Nova Scotia, St. John's, Oct. 26, 1828, Cormack Papers; Howley, *Beothucks*, 208.

166   Wm. Creed to W.E. Cormack, Aug. 30, 1827, Cormack Papers, https://collections.mun.ca/digital/collection/archives/id/10650/rec/86.

167   John Louis was probably recruited by Mr. Creed, Galtois, letters from Creed to W.E. Cormack, Aug. 30, 1827, and Sept. 3, 1827, Cormack Papers, https://collections.mun.ca/digital/collection/archives/id/10650/rec/86 and https://collections.mun.ca/digital/collection/archives/id/10313/rec/87.

168   Howley, *Beothucks*, 279, n.1; Noel Mathews, one of Howley's Mi'kmaw canoe-men, had learned that from old Maurice Louis, the chief of his tribe, who accompanied Cormack in 1827 on his trip to Red Indian Lake.

169   Also spelled John Stephens; he was recruited at Clode Sound, Cormack Papers; Howley, *Beothucks*, 216.

170   John Stark Nova Scotia to W.E. Cormack, Halifax, Dec. 21, 1827, Cormack Papers, https://collections.mun.ca/digital/collection/archives/id/10577/rec/80; Howley, *Beothucks*, 207.

171   Cormack Papers, "Sylvester Grumble," probably written in 1827.

172   Cormack sailed on Jan. 14, 1828, after the search for Beothuk survivors: *Public Ledger*, Jan. 15, 1828.

173   Cormack, "Mr. Cormack's Journey," 318–29.

174   Howley, *Beothucks*, 189–97.

175   The museum had been founded by Jameson. The items donated by Cormack are listed in the Day Record Book for Mar. 15, 1828, and the Week Record Book for Mar. 15, 1828, of the University Museum, now in the archive of the National Museums Scotland. Several of the listed items are no longer in the collection. Two birchbark containers were transferred to the British Museum in 1870 (J.C.H. King, curator at the British Museum, personal communication with Marshall, 1978); it is believed that a Beothuk coat fringe (no. 2583) in the British Museum was also taken by Cormack from the "Chief's Tomb."

176   *Public Ledger*, Jan. 15, 1828, 2–3: Cormack sailed on the brigantine *Geo Canning; The Newfoundlander*, May 22, 1828: Cormack arrived back in St. John's.

177   John Stark to W.E. Cormack, Dec. 21, 1827; Howley, *Beothucks*, 200.

178   W.E. Cormack to John Stark, Oct. 26, 1827, https://collections.mun.ca/digital/collection/archives/id/10339/rec/74; Howley, *Beothucks*, 197.

179   Stark to Cormack, May 28, 2828, https://collections.mun.ca/digital/collection/archives/id/10287/rec/81; Howley, *Beothucks*, 201.

180   Instructions by W.E. Cormack, president of the Boeothick Institution; Howley, *Beothucks*, 216.

181   Cormack to Stark, May 24, 1828; Howley, *Beothucks*, 199.

182   Cormack to Stark, June 21, 1828; Howley, *Beothucks*, 200.

183   Howley, *Beothucks*, 217.

184   Howley, *Beothucks*, 219–20.

185   Bishop John Inglis to W.E. Cormack, Nov. 13, 1828; Howley, *Beothucks*, 209; John Stark to W.E. Cormack, Sept. 12, 1828; Howley, *Beothucks*, 201.

186   John Stark to Cormack, Sept. 16, 1828, Cormack Papers.

187   Amy Louise Peyton to *The Evening Telegram*, Feb. 12, 1986; John and Eleanor Peyton were married in February 1823.

188   Howley, *Beothucks*, 175.

189   Newfoundland Provincial Reference and Resource Library (PRRL), 917.18 C81 NRV, W.E. Cormack to John Peyton Jr., St. John's, Oct. 28, 1828; Howley, *Beothucks*, 225.

190   Shanawdithit's Sketch V, The Rooms Museum, NF 3308; Howley, *Beothucks*, 245.

191   C.R. Fay, *Life and Labour in Newfoundland* (Toronto: Toronto University Press, 1956), 101.

192   PRRL, 917.18 C81 NRV, W.E. Cormack to John Peyton Jr., St. John's, Oct. 28, 1828.

193   Stark to Cormack, Sept. 16, 1828, Cormack Papers; Howley, *Beothucks*, 202.

194   This note is preserved in the Cormack Papers; Howley, *Beothucks*, 203.

195   TNA, UK, CO 194/81, ff. 59a–60, Dr. William Carson, "Answers to Questions by the Royal College of Physicians of Great Britain, 1830," attached to Governor Cochrane's letter to Viscount Goderich, Feb. 7, 1831.

196   TNA, UK, CO 194/81, ff. 59a–60, Carson, "Answers to Questions."

197   Howley, *Beothucks*, 196; Marshall, *History*, 204–7.

198   Anonymous (John MacGregor), "Sketches of Savage Life, No. II, Shaa-naan-dithit, or the last of the Boeothics," *Frazer's Magazine for Town and Country* 13, no. 75 (1836): 322.

199   Bishop John Inglis diary, 4.7.1827 (Can) N.S. 9, doc. 57–58, USPG.

200   Inglis diary, 4.7.1827 (Can) N.S. 9, doc. 57–58, USPG.

201   Howley, *Beothucks*, 225.

202   "Sketches of Savage Life," 322.

203   "Sketches of Savage Life," 322.

204   Carson, "Answers to Questions"; TNA, UK, CO 194/81, ff. 59a–60.

205   Cormack Papers; Howley, *Beothucks*, 225.

206   The Rooms Museum, Shanawdithit's Sketch I, NF 3305; Howley, *Beothucks*, 239.

207   The Rooms Museum, Shanawdithit's Sketch II, NF 3304; Howley, *Beothucks*, 240.

208   The Rooms Museum, Shanawdithit's Sketch III, NF 3306; Howley, *Beothucks*, 241.

209   The Rooms Museum, Shanawdithit's Sketch V, NF 3308; Howley, *Beothucks*, 245.

210   Howley, *Beothucks*, 244–45.

211   Howley, *Beothucks*, 226–27; Cormack Papers.

212   The Rooms Museum, Shanawdithit's Sketch VI, NF 3309; Howley, *Beothucks*, 246.

213   The Rooms Museum, Shanawdithit's Sketch VII, NF 3310; Howley, *Beothucks*, 246.

214   The Rooms Museum, Shanawdithit's Sketch VIII, NF 3311; Howley, *Beothucks*, 248.

215   The Rooms Museum, Shanawdithit's Sketch X, NF 3313; Howley, *Beothucks*, 249.

216   The Rooms Museum, Shanawdithit's Sketch IX, NF 3312; Howley, *Beothucks*, 249. Letter, Cormack to Bishop John Inglis, St. John's, Oct. 26, 1828, Howley, *Beothucks*, 209.

217   Oubee was captured in 1791 and taken in by Mr. Stone's family; she was later taken by them to Britain and died there in or before 1795. In 1792, Capt. George C. Pulling obtained from her a list of 111 Beothuk words. Ingeborg Marshall, *Reports and Letters by George Christopher Pulling Relating to the Beothuk Indians of Newfoundland* (St. John's: Breakwater, 1989), 26, 113–18.

218   John Hewson, *Beothuk Vocabularies* (St. John's: Technical Papers of the Newfoundland Museum, 1978), 149–67.

219   Archives of the Natural History Society of Montreal, McCord Museum, Redpath Library Building, Blacker-Wood Library, Montreal, Minutes of a meeting of the Society on Feb. 23, 1829, recording the reading of a letter from W.E. Cormack, Jan. 10, 1829, St. John's, Newfoundland.

220   *Dictionary of National Biography*, s.v. "Yates, James," http://www.oxforddnb.com/view/article/30192?docPos=2. James Yates, antiquarian, fellow of the Geological, Linnean, and Royal Societies and secretary to the council of the British Association, went to Glasgow University in 1811. For further details, see Marshall, *History*, 432–33.

221   Joseph Noad, Lecture on the *Aborigines of Newfoundland* (St. John's: R.J. Parsons, 1859), 34–35.

222   Howley, *Beothucks*, 131; Dr. Rick Cooper, St. John's, personal communication with author, 2013.

223   J.K. Kent to John Peyton, St. John's, June 12, 1829, PANL, C.F. Rowe Collection MG 134; Carson, "Answers to Questions."

224   Royal College of Surgeons to J. Laws Esq. Jan. 29, 1953, CNS, file Shanawdithit.

225   Howley, *Beothucks*, 231–32.

226   Shanawdithit's burial certificate, written by Frederic H. Carrington, has: "1829, Nancy Shanadith, Buried South Side, ? , 23rd," Howley Family Papers, MUN Archives and Special Collections, COLL-262, QEII Library. Entry in the Cathedral of St. John the Baptist Diocese of Eastern Newfoundland and Labrador Register of Burials, Jan. 1, 1825, to Dec. 17, 1845, CA 1/4/3: "8th June Nancy Shanadithi at. [age] 23, South Side (very probably the last of the aborigines)."

227   Marshall, *History*, 220–21; Cormack Papers.

228   Cormack Papers.

229   Cormack Papers.

230   J.G. Whittier, "The Indian Girl's Lament," in *The Literary Souvenir*, ed. Alaric A. Watts (London: Longman, 1831), 134–37.

231   *The Public Ledger*, Apr., May, Nov. 1827; Apr., May, June 1828; *The Royal Gazette*, Apr., May 1828.

232   *The Public Ledger*, May 1, 1827; Apr.–May 1828.

233   *The Public Ledger*, July 3, 1827, J. Clift, Auctioneer; see also Nov. 1827; May, June 1828; *The Royal Gazette*, Apr., May 1828.

234   *The Public Ledger*, May 12, 19, 1829.

235   The Royal Gazette, Jan.–Apr. 1828; *The Public Ledger*, Jan.–Mar. 1828. On Noad's *Plan of St. John's*, Thomson's heirs are listed as owning the waterfront premises to the west of Roope's Plantation, TRPAD, MG 93, William Noad collection.

236   *The Public Ledger*, Jan. 15, 1828, on the *George Canning*.

237   *The Royal Gazette*. The advertisement ran from May to December 1828.

238   *The Royal Gazette,* May 12, 19, 1828. Auctions were to be held on the 14th and 19th of the month.

239   *The Public Ledger*, May and June 1828 (ale); Sept. 19, 23, 1828 (snuff).

240   *The Public Ledger*, Jan. 23, 1829.

241   MHA, name file "Cormack."

242   *The Public Ledger*, May 29, 1829.

243   *The Public Ledger,* May 8 to June 16, 1829, list of items June 19.

244   *The Royal Gazette,* May 26, 1829.

245   *The Royal Gazette,* June 9, 1829.

246   *The Royal Gazette,* Oct. 27, throughout November and until December 8, 1829. *The Newfoundlander,* Oct. 29, 1829.

247   MHA, name file "Cormack."

248   *Prince Edward Island Register* (Charlottetown), Sept. 15, 1829, 3. The sale included, in Charlottetown, town lot no. 70, half town lots no. 8 and no. 9. There were also pasture lots nos. 354, 549, and 556 in one area, and pasture lots nos. 200, 241, 250, 256, and 277 in another area, covering 72 acres.

249   *The Public Ledger,* May 11, 14, 18, 21, 25, 1830.

250   Newfoundland and Labrador Registry of Deeds, Service NL Commercial Registration, St. John's, vol. 9, pp. 9–10. On Nov. 1, 1833, David S. Rennie purchased James Gower's share.

251   *The Royal Gazette,* July 19, 1831; Aug. 2, 1831.

252   According to the *Numeric Index,* the lots included 11 dwelling houses, three stores, two gardens, a forge, and a property of unknown use.

253   TRPAD, MG 93, William R. Noad Collection, *Plan of St. John's* and 1853 *Numeric Index.*

254   Will of Charles Scott (one of William and Janet Grace Scott's sons), who died on Jan. 1, 1921, mentions "The Scott and Rennie Estate" concerning property in Newfoundland; TRPAD, MG 93, William R. Noad Collection, *Plan of St. John's* and 1853 *Numeric Index.*

255   Parish of St. Pancras in the Co. of Middlesex, Baptismal Register, Mar. 20, 1833, no. 437, Anna Janet: John Bell and Mary Ann Cormack, Johnson Street, Writer to the Signet, "said to be born 13 January 1831."

256   Edinburgh Parish Register OPR 685.1/64: "Proclaimed 22nd [Apr. 1832] John Bell Cormack Esq. W.S. in Hill St., St. George's Parish &; Miss Mary Ann Crawfuird daur. of the late Allan Crawfuird of Kingston Jamaica residing in Queensferry Street same Parish 3P. No objections. Married 27 April by the Revd. James Martin of St George's."

257   TRPAD, Rennie-McNamara Collection, box I: Letters—London and Liverpool. John Bell Cormack, Dec. 11, 1832, to David S. Rennie, and Feb. 27, 1833, London, at Messrs Scotts, 27 Austin Friars, to David S. Rennie.

258   David Stuart Rennie studied law at Edinburgh University from 1831 to 1833, Edinburgh University Matriculation Roll: Arts, Law, Divinity, III: 1811–1829, David Rennie, Edinburgh: 1 Law p. 1062 (1831), 2 Law p. 1092 (1832), 3 Law, p. 1836 (1836).

259   TRPAD, Rennie-McNamara Collection, box I: Letters—London and Liverpool. John Bell Cormack, Feb. 27, 1833, London, at Messrs. Scotts, 27 Austin Friars, to David S. Rennie. The address suggests that the couple was assisted by Janet Grace Scott; they had a second child, Alexander William, in January 1833, Parish of St. Pancras in the Co. of Middlesex, Baptismal register, Mar. 20, 1833, No. 438.

260   *The Royal Gazette,* July 12, 1836.

261   PARO PEI, RS 16, Liber 44, f. 156, 159, Sept. 9, 1836.

262   Newfoundland and Labrador Registry of Deeds, Central District, 11/255: John Bell Cormack sold his share of the land [farm] on June 19, 1848 to Kenneth McLea, Sr.; 11/544: John Bell Cormack sold his share of the land [Victoria Park area] on October 3, 1849, to Charles Fox Bennett. The tracts of land were not part of Roope's Plantation and were situated beyond the boundary of Noad's plan.

263   *The Royal Gazette*, July 12, 1836, vol. 6, no. 310; PARO PEI, RG 16, Liber 44, ff. 156, 159, Sept. 9, 1836. He died in St. John's on Feb. 8, 1869, *The Royal Gazette and Newfoundland Advertiser*, vol. 62, no. 7 (Feb. 16, 1869).

264   W.E. Cormack to Sir George Murray, Secretary of State for the Colonial Department, May 18, 1829, TNA UK. CO 194/79 ff. 159–161; "Of Newfoundland" in Cormack's hand, no date; CO 194/79, f. 171; Cormack to Murray, July 8, 1829; Sept. 1829, CO 194/79, f. 184; Cormack to Murray, Sept. 17, 1829; CO 194/79, ff. 186–87; Cormack to Murray, n.d.; 194/80, f. 354.

265   National Library of Scotland, Edinburgh, Murray Papers, Adv. Ms. 46.8.14, p. 82, A. Weddesburn (for Murray) to Cormack, Jan. 12, 1830, holding out for a job; p. 309, June 4, 1830, no job available. Murray's reasons for rejecting Cormack's bid for a job though he was highly qualified may have been of a personal nature, as he removed Cormack's last two letters to him from the government correspondence into his personal papers.

266   *British Columbian*, May 9, 1868, Obituary of W.E. Cormack; Howley, *Beothucks*, 235.

267   Natural History Society Archives, McCord Museum, Redpath Library Building, Blacker-Wood Library, Montreal, Minutes of a meeting of the Natural History Society of Montreal on Apr. 25, 1831.

268   Natural History Society Archives, McCord Museum, Redpath Library Building, Blacker-Wood Library, Montreal Minutes of the Natural History Society of Montreal, meetings on Apr. 25, Nov. 28, 1831; Oct. 29, 1832; Dec. 27, 1852; *Montreal Gazette*, Nov. 13, 1832.

269   TNA, UK, Board of Trade, No. 42941, BT 1/265. TNA UK, CO 194/79, ff. 186–87. In September 1829, Cormack left a copy of the paper at the offce of Sir George Murray, Secretary of State for the Colonies. This was most likely an unexpurgated version. The paper is still on file in the Board of Trade papers in The National Archives, Kew.

270   Cormack, "Account of a Journey."

271   "Narrative of a Journey across Newfoundland by W.E. Cormack (For the Natural History Society of Montreal)." McCord Museum, Redpath Library Building, Blacker-Wood Library, Cormack Journal (M4511). The exact date when Cormack wrote the manuscript is not known—the watermark on most pages is 1830; a few pages are marked 1827. Pages 1, 12, 40–49 are written in a different hand.

272   Dr. Joyce Macpherson, personal communication with author, 2005.

273   Royal Botanic Gardens, Kew, Library and Archives, Director's Correspondence, vol. 43, doc. 25, pp. 55–56, Robert Morison, May 30, 1824, to Sir William Hooker; Hugh Clapperton, *Journal of a Second Expedition*, 1829 (London: John Murray, 1966), xiv.

274   Royal Botanic Gardens, Kew, Library and Archives, Director's Correspondence, vol. 43, doc. 25, pp. 55–56, Robert Morison, May 30, 1824, to Sir William Hooker; Miscellaneous Letters 1818/30, XLIV (55), W.E. Cormack to Sir William Hooker, Newfoundland, Jan. 10, 1825.

275   Royal Botanic Gardens, Miscellaneous Letters 1818/30, XLIV (55), Cormack to Hooker, Newfoundland, Jan. 10, 1825.

276   Royal Botanic Gardens, Directors' Correspondence, Robert Morison to Sir William Hooker, May 30, 1824, vol. 43, doc. 25, pp. 55–56; Morison to Hooker, Jan. 10, 1825, vol. 44, doc. 94, p. 178.

277   In his correspondence with Cormack, Hooker asked him for advice with regard to a gentleman who was to come to Newfoundland to conduct botanical research. Royal Botanical Gardens, Miscellaneous Letters 1818/1830 XLIV (55), Cormack to Hooker, Jan. 10, 1825.

278   Glasgow Street Directories from 1819 to 1827 list David Rennie's home on West Bath Street, which was also the address of Sir William Hooker. According to the Minute Books of Glasgow Sheriff Court Register of Deeds, 1821, SC 36/65/23, ff. xxxviii–xliiii, Hooker's property in Bath Street bordered on that owned by David Rennie.

279   According to the author of Cormack's obituary, Cormack frequently sent specimens of plants to the Linnean Society in Britain (between 1819 and 1834), though neither plants nor any correspondence with Cormack has survived in the records of this society: Gina Douglas, Librarian and Archivist, The Linnean Society of London, personal communication with author, Feb. 11, 1997.

280   The catalogue of vascular plant specimens produced by Dr. E. Rouleau, Director of the Botanical Institute of the University of Montreal, in the 1960s, under contract by the Agnes Marion Ayre Herbarium of Memorial University of Newfoundland, has 21 plants listed for the Herbarium at the Royal Botanic Gardens, Kew. However, despite a lengthy correspondence with its archivist, Lesley Price, in 1998, it was not possible to establish any of these plants in the present collection.

281   Of the two plants listed in Dr. E. Rouleau's catalogue of known species of Newfoundland vascular plants as being in the Grey Herbarium collection, only one plant, *Leontodon autumnalis*, is still present: Sharon Yelton, Harvard University Herbaria, personal communication with author, Mar. 12, 2001. Her letter included photocopies of photographs of the plant and of the label of the specimen.

282   Provincial Archives of New Brunswick (hereafter PANB), Correspondence with M. Currie, Public Service Archivist, Mar. 1998.

283   PARO PEI, 2316.2, pp. 18–23, Robert Stewart to Geo. R. Young, 94 Russel Str. (London, UK), Sept. 3, 1834. Young claimed that Cormack, during an election for a new MHA for which his brother was a candidate, "went among the highlanders in a tartan waistcoat" and called himself MacCormack (denied by Cormack) to get votes for Mr. Smith, an agent of the Mining Company; Public Archives of British Columbia (hereafter PABC), F. 364a.2, W.E. Cormack to Lieut. Gov. Moody, Victoria, Feb. 16, 1859.

284   *The Royal Gazette*, Nov. 8, 1831, 3.

285   PANB, RS 108, Land Petitions Series, 1833, W.E. Cormack.

286   *The Royal Gazette*, Nov. 8, 1833, 3; *The Novascotian*, July 16, 1834, 3–4; *The Chatham Gleaner*, July 22, 1834.

287   PARO PEI, 2316.2, pp. 522–27, Robert Stewart to Geo. R. Young, 94 Russel Str. (London, UK), 3 Dec. 1836; State Archives of New South Wales (hereafter SANSW), A.O.N.S.W. COD 33, Passenger list of barque *Clarinda*, left London May 7, 1836, arrived at Port Jackson Sept. 14, 1836: Cormack was the only passenger.

288   Bernard D. Fardy, *William Epps Cormack Newfoundland Pioneer* (St. John's: Creative, 1985).

289   Passenger list of barque *Clarinda*, Sept. 14, 1836 A.O.N.S.W. COD 33, SANSWA.

290   Letter by Cormack to Governor Gipps of New South Wales, Aust. July 30, 1838. Top No. 1939/1315 Ref: A.O.N.S.W. 4/2472.2, SANSWA.

291   Letter by Police Magistrate Cook to Postmaster General Raymond, July 17, 1838. Top No. 1839/1315 Ref: A.O.N.S.W. 4/2472.2, SANSWA.

292   Letter by Cormack to Raymond, July 2, 1838. Top No. 1839/1315 Ref: A.O.N.S.W. 4/2472.2, SANSWA.

293   Letter by Raymond to Gipps, June 27, 1839. Top No. 1839/1315 Ref: A.O.N.S.W. 4/2472.2, SANSWA.

294   "Householder's Return," Return No. 68, X946, p. 129, SANSWA.

295   Thirty years later, Dungog supported two tobacco "manufactories" and the cultivation of the weed had been entered into quite extensively. The groundwork Cormack had laid at his 1839 farm at East Bend had flourished, once again proving him to be a man of vision. *Ballier's New Gazetteer*, New South Wales, Australia, 1866. SANSWA.

296   Cormack's Deposition to Court at Stroud, May 7, 1839. Top No. 1839/5471 Ref: A.O.N.S.W. 4/2454.3, SANSWA.

297   Cormack's Deposition to Court at Stroud, May 7, 1839. Top No. 1839/5471 Ref: A.O.N.S.W. 4/2454.3, SANSWA. Cormack also stated that two days after he returned to Stroud, Parnell was again suspended from the constabulary for improper conduct. A likely cause was his having lost his prisoner after swimming the William's River. Letter by Cormack to Gipps, May 7, 1839. Top No. 1839/5471 Ref: A.O.N.S.W. 4/2454.3, SANSWA.

298   Fardy, *William Epps Cormack*, 46.

299   James Rowe and Margaret A. Rowe, *New Zealand* (London: Ernest Benn Ltd., 1968), 44.

300   C.W. Vennell and David More, *Land of the Three Rivers, A Continental History of Piako County* (Auckland, NZ: Wilson & Horton Ltd., 1976), 38–40. *NSW Government Gazette*, 1841, Sydney, Mar. 16, 1841, "New Zealand," pp. 382–83, case 73: five parcels of land claimed by W.E. Cormack of Sydney, in New Zealand on the Pararu, Piako, and Waipa rivers; pp. 375–76, cases 144, 147, 149, 150, 151. Cormack is listed as agent for the land purchasers; Cormack's claim for himself, case 178, p. 482.

301   Fardy, *William Epps Cormack*, 47.

302   Rowe and Rowe, *New Zealand*, 42.

303   Letter, Cormack to the Marquis of Breadalbane, Aug. 15, 1845. Ref: GD 112/61/1 Public Record Office, Edinburgh, Scotland.

304   Letter, Cormack to the Marquis of Breadalbane, Aug. 15, 1845.

305   Letter, Cormack to the Marquis of Breadalbane, Aug. 15, 1845.

306   Letter, Cormack to Gipps, April 24, 1841. Top No. 1841/4505 Ref: A.O.N.S.W. 4/2543.1 SANSWA.

307   Auckland Provincial Centennial Council, 1940. "Roll of Early Settlers in Auckland Province Prior to end of 1852." Alexander Turnbull Library, Wellington, New Zealand, Dec. 20, 1978, Fardy, personal communication with NZ library.

308   The Hoken Library, University of Otago, Dunedin, NZ, correspondence with D.C.

MacDonald, Reference Librarian, May 7, 1984; Ingeborg Marshall Collection, MUN Library Archives and Special Collections, COLL-496.

309   Una Platts, *The Lively Capital: Auckland 1840–1865* (Christchurch, NZ: Avon Fine Prints, 1971), 35.

310   "Preliminary Inventory No. 9: Old Land Claims." File OLC 143-144 National Archives of New Zealand, Wellington, New Zealand (hereafter NANZ).

311   Letter, Cormack to Donald McLean, Crown Lands Commissioner of New Zealand, Nov. 19, 1844. Ms. Papers 32. f. 231 Alexander Turnbull Library, Wellington, New Zealand (hereafter ATLNZ).

312   Letter, Cormack to John McKay, Mar. 6, 1843. Top No. 1843/6008 SANSWA.

313   TNA, UK, CO 209, vol. 20 Index, 20 Mar. 1843, Mr. Willis's petition on Land Claim. TNA, UK, CO 361, vol. 1, 1849–1851, Mar. 22, 1850, No. 2194, Claim to Land on Piako River, Messrs. W.E. Cormack, Henry H. Willis, Tho. Garret, and G. Silver for four distinct positions.

314   NRS, GD 112/61/10, W.E. Cormack to the Marquis of Breadalbane, Taymouth Castle. The Marquis of Breadalbane had been a classmate of Cormack at the University of Glasgow, 1812–13, Glasgow University Archives, Class Catalogues, 1794–1838 [R9/1/1].

315   Letter, Cormack to Marquis of Breadalbane, Aug. 15, 1845. Ref: GD 112/61/1 Public Record Office, Edinburgh, Scotland.

316   Royal Botanic Gardens, Kew, Library and Archives, English Letters, A–H, 1843, XIX (159), W.E. Cormack to Sir William Hooker, May 27, 1843, at Mr. Willis, Crosby Square. Cormack had travelled on business to Sydney and from there unexpectedly took a boat to Great Britain. He is unlikely to have carried his Newfoundland papers with him at that time.

317   Cormack Papers, "Of the Red Indians of Newfoundland," watermarks Superfine 1840, Chafford Mills 1843; Cormack Papers, "Geology and Mineralogy," watermark Chafford Mills, 1843.

318   Frank S.J.L. James, ed., *The Correspondence of Michael Faraday* (London: Institution of Electrical Engineers, 1996), Vol. 3, 1841–December 1848, Letters 1334–2145.

319   Depositions at Court Hearings, June 14, 1844, file OLC 143-144 NANZ.

320   Cormack to McLean, Apr. 11, 1847. Ms. papers 32, f. 231 ATLNZ. To make things all the more difficult, in 1845 Governor Grey had demanded that all land claims such as Cormack's be verified by deeds, maps, and surveys and copies sent to the Lands Commissioner by Sept. 15, 1846, or such claims would not be considered by the review to be held of them later that year. It was "an attempt to induce these purchasers to abandon or compromise their claims." "Preliminary Inventory No. 9: Old Land Claims," p. 3, file OLC 143-144 NANZ.

321   Royal Botanic Gardens, Kew, Library and Archives, English Letters, 1851 XXI (134), W.E. Cormack to Sir William Hooker, Mar. 1851.

322   McLean to Cormack, Aug. 26, 1845. Ms. papers 32, f. 231 ATLNZ.

323   Alexander Turnbull Library, Wellington, NZ, Ms. paper 32, folder 321, Donald McLean to W.E. Cormack, Aug. 26, 1845.

324   Cormack to Governor Fitzroy of New Zealand, July 19, 1844, file OLC 143-144 NANZ.

325   Rowe and Rowe, *New Zealand*, 46.

326   TNA, UK, CO 406, vol. 10, f. 203 (99), Apr. 27, 1850, B. Hawes on behalf of Earl Grey to W.E. Cormack "and others" respecting their "alleged claim."

327   TNA UK, CO 406, vol. 11, f. 280 (138), July 12, 1851, B. Hawes on behalf of Earl Grey to W.E. Cormack "and others." Grey refused to interfere with the decision by the proper authority. For more information on the developments in New Zealand and Cormack's adversaries, see Fardy, *William Epps Cormack*, 46–62.

328   Royal Botanic Gardens, Kew, Library and Archives, English Letters, 1851 XXI (134), W.E. Cormack to Sir William Hooker, Mar. 1851.

329   Natural History Museum, Department of Library and Information Services, London, Owen Collection, pp. 426–32, W.E. Cormack to Professor Owen, Oct. 18 and 25, 1850; Richard Owen, *Memoirs on the Extinct Wingless Birds of New Zealand: With an Appendix on Those of England, Australia, Newfoundland, Mauritius and Rodriguez* (England: J. Van Voorst, 1879), 220.

330   *The British Columbian* (New Westminster, BC), Jan. 16, 1862, 3.

331   R. S. Jones, *The Art of Skating Practically Explained, by Lieut. R. Jones, R.S. with Revisions and Additions by W.E. Cormack, Esq.* (London: Bailey Brothers, 3 Royal Exchange Buildings, [1855]). The booklet was republished in 1865 with only the name of Robert Jones given as the author. Having searched in the Union Catalogue, Utlas, Amicus, and OCLC, the only library found with a copy of the 1855 edition is the Springfield College Babson Library in Springfield, MA.

332   Robert Jones, *A Treatise on Skating: Founded on Certain Principles Deduced from Many Years of Experience* (London: J. Ridley, 1772). It was reprinted in 1774, 1780, and 1797, and reprints in 1823 and 1825 were published with the title *The Art of Skating* (London: William Cole, 10 Newgate Street).

333   The figures—all male—wore top hats, dress shirts and bow tie, waistcoats, dress coats, and pants as worn in the 1850s.

334   Royal Botanic Gardens, Kew, Library and Archives, English Letters, 1851, XXXI (134) W.E. Cormack to Sir William Hooker, Mar. 1851.

335   Howley, *Beothucks*, 220–230.

336   Howley, *Beothucks*, 220, 231.

337   *The Royal Gazette and Newfoundland Advertiser*, Jan. 18, 1853, 3; *The Patriot and Terra Nova Herald*, Jan. 22, 1853, 3; *The Morning Courier*, Jan. 19, 1853, 2.

338   Joseph Noad, *The Aborigines of Newfoundland—the Red Indians* (St. John's: The Patriot Press, 1853). This 50-page booklet was republished in 1859, in St. John's by R.J. Parsons, Printer.

339   TNA, UK, CO 194/148, ff. 406–7, Governor C.H. Darling to Henry Labouchere M.P., Oct. 1856.

340   *The Weekly Dispatch* (London), Jan. 6, 1850, "The Californian Constitution."

341   Royal Botanic Gardens, Kew, Library and Archives, English Letters, 1851, XXXI (134), W.E. Cormack to Sir William Hooker, Mar. 1851; Passenger list, *Daily Alta California*, Oct. 6, 1851. The vessel sailed from Panama on Sept. 15.

342   City Directory Records, San Francisco, 1854–1858. San Francisco Public Library, San Francisco, California. Bernard Fardy, personal correspondence with San Franscisco Public Library, November 2, 1978. City Directories list the firm of Smith & Bros. as being at the

northwest corner of California and Battery streets; also lists Cormack's residence at 118 Sacramento Street from 1854 to 1858.

343   William Webber Johnson, *The Forty-Niners* (New York: Time-Life Books, 1974).

344   Fardy, *William Epps Cormack*, 66.

345   Internet site "Ancestry"; *San Francisco City Directories* for 1856–58, letter from the California Historical Society, 678 Mission Street, San Francisco, Mar. 2, 2001. Fardy, *William Epps Cormack*, 64.

346   Johnson, *Forty-Niners*.

347   Fardy, *William Epps Cormack*, 66.

348   Letter, M.W. Cromartie to Governor Douglas, Feb. 15, 1859, PABC.

349   Letter, Cormack to Douglas, Mar. 10, 1860, PABC.

350   Letter, Cormack to Douglas, Mar. 10, 1860.

351   Stephen Franklin, *The Heroes* (Toronto: McLellan and Stewart, 1967), 114.

352   *The British Colonist*, July 20, 1859, PABC.

353   TNA, UK, C 60, v. 13, ff. 345–349, July 28, 1862, Cormack, chairman, and John Rochfort Umiacke, secretary: "to the Queen's most Excellent Majesty, In Council, the Lords Spiritual and Temporal of the United Kingdom of Great Britain and Ireland in Parliament assembled. To the Honorable the Commons of the United Kingdom of Great Britain and Ireland in Parliament assembled."

354   Letter, Cormack to Colonial Secretary, Jan. 25, 1862, PABC.

355   W.E. Cormack, *On the Fisheries of North America*, manuscript in PABC.

356   Fardy, *William Epps Cormack*, 73.

357   *British Columbian*, Feb. 13, 21, 1861; *New Westminster Times*, Jan. 5,1861, PABC.

358   Letter, Cormack to Lt. Gov. Col. Moody, Mar. 18, 1861, PABC.

359   Fardy, *William Epps Cormack*, 74.

360   Letter, Cormack to H. Pillew Crease, Jan. 23, 1862, PABC.

361   *British Columbian*, May 9, 1868, PABC.

362   *British Columbian*, May 9, 1868, Obituary of W.E. Cormack; Howley, Beothucks, 236

363   *British Columbian*, June 7, 1862, letter to the editor.

364   *British Colonist*, Oct. 31, 1863, PABC.

365   *British Colonist*, Nov. 4, 1863, PABC.

366   *British Columbian*, May 9, 1868. If this scheme seems to be rather extraordinary, it should be mentioned that another such scheme saw the interbreeding of cattle and buffalo about thirty years later that resulted in the birth of a beast called the "cattalo." The experiment soon folded, not because it was unsuccessful, but because of expense and lack of technology. Indeed, that same interbreeding of cattle and buffalo is an ongoing concern today, the beast being produced going by its new 20th century name of "beefalo." Fardy, *William Epps Cormack*, 75.

367   Letter, Cormack to colonial government, BC, July 29, 1864, PABC.

368   Letters, Cormack to colonial government, BC, Nov. 4, 29, 1867, PABC.

369   Howley, *Beothucks*, 236–37.

370   Fay, *Life and Labour*, 91.

371   Howley, *Beothucks*, 236–237.

372   Cormack, *Narrative*. Bruton questioned the authenticity of the photograph of Cormack that is now widely used and therefore did not include it in his publication. PRRL, Catalog, Box 5, item 53, Dec. 19, 1928, Ernest C. Finch to Mr. Rennie.

373   Tom Furlong, "Remembering a Historic Trek," *The Telegram*, Sept. 20, 2003; *Newfoundland and Labrador Studies* (2010): 335, 339, 410.

374   PRRL, M-25, Rennie Papers, file 4, R.J. Rennie to Miss Morris, Sept. 29, 1931, and Miss Ella Morris to R.J. Rennie, Sept. 29, 1931.

375   *Gazetteer of Canada: Newfoundland and Labrador*, 1st ed. (Ottawa, 1968), 47.

376   *Encyclopedia of Newfoundland and Labrador*, s.v. "Cormack."

377   Cormack Academy, Stephenville; Cormack Street in Labrador City; Cormack Square, Cormack Bridge, and Cormack Mini Mart in Milton, photographed by Ingeborg Marshall; Cormack Drive and Cormack Realty in Clarenville; according to former City Clerk Rupert Green, who was at the time on the Nomenclature Board, Cormack Street in St. John's was named after W.E. Cormack and not after Hon. James Cormack (1799–1869) of the Legislative Council (personal communication, May 15, 1998).

378   *Newfoundland Travel Guide* (St. John's, NL: Dept. of Development and Tourism, Government of Newfoundland and Labrador, 1998), 40.

379   Howley, *Beothucks*, 144.

380   Don Cayo and Ray Fennelly, "Crossing the Rock," *Canadian Geographic* (1992): 38–49.

381   Furlong, "Remembering a Historic Trek."

382   N.R. Williams, "Cormack's Trail Retraced," read before the Newfoundland Historical Society, St. John's, May 28, 1971, manuscript in CNS.

383   Chris Flannagan, "Platoon Travels Historic Route," *The Evening Telegram*, Sept. 17, 1994, 1; "Bears Get Meal at Soldier's Expense," *The Evening Telegram*, 23 Oct. 1994, 3.

384   "Mr. Knowling's Tramp Through the Country," *The Trade Review* (St. John's), Apr. 16, 1904; John Lewis, "The Island in Winter," ms. copy in the possession of author. Lewis crossed the island on skis in seven stages, between 1975 and 1985.

385   *The Royal City Record* (New Westminster), Aug. 16, 1986.

386   Randy Joyce, "Fund Inaugurated to Provide Monument for Cormack's Grave in B.C. Community," *The Evening Telegram*, Aug. 16, 1977.

387   Archie Miller, curator of the New Westminster Museum, to author, June 2, 1998.

388   The date of Cormack's death was recorded on the headstone as April 29, 1868; Joyce, "Fund Inaugurated."

389   *The Royal City Record* (New Westminster), Aug. 16, 1986. Information about the memorial and a copy of the photograph and inscription were provided by the curator of the museum, Archie Miller.

390   Inscription copied from the memorial by author.

391   *British Columbian*, May 9, 1868; Howley, *Beothucks*, 234–37. It is believed that John Robson, editor of the British Columbian, was the author of the obituary. Edward Graham to the editor of *The Public Ledger* (Newfoundland), Victoria, BC, Sept. 20, 1871, published in *The Public Ledger*, Oct. 31, 1871.

About the Author

Ingeborg Marshall was born in 1929 in East Germany. She fled with her family to West Germany at the end of the Second World War, and went on to study German and English Literature at Hamburg University, and on a scholarship to study and teach at Bucknell University, Pennsylvania, and Sarah Lawrence College in New York. In 1961 she married Dr. William Marshall. After several years in London, Melbourne, Australia, and New York, the Marshalls, now with three children, moved to Newfoundland in 1968. Marshall soon became fascinated by the Beothuk and began the academic work she would become renowned for.

In 1984 Marshall received a Masters of Anthropology from Memorial University. Her thesis, *Beothuk Bark Canoes: An Analysis and Comparative Study* was published by the National Museum. Her research has included archaeological surveys of Beothuk camp and burial sites and a systematic search for previously uncovered documents about the Beothuk. She published *The Beothuk of Newfoundland: a Vanished People,* used as a textbook in schools; *A History and Ethnography of the Beothuk,* an exhaustive and essential reference on the Beothuk; and the paperback *The Beothuk.* In 2005 she received the Order of Newfoundland and Labrador and in 2006 an honorary doctorate from Memorial University of Newfoundland.